Islamic Philosophy

A Beginner's Guide

T0056921

ONEWORLD BEGINNER'S GUIDES combine an original, inventive, and engaging approach with expert analysis on subjects ranging from art and history to religion and politics, and everything in-between. Innovative and affordable, books in the series are perfect for anyone curious about the way the world works and the big ideas of our time.

aesthetics
africa
american politics
anarchism
animal behaviour
anthropology
anti-capitalism
aquinas
archaeology
art
artificial intelligence
the baha'i faith
the beat generation
the bible
biodiversity
bioterror & biowarfare
the brain
british politics
the Buddha
cancer
censorship
christianity
civil liberties
classical music
climate change
cloning
the cold war
conservation
crimes against humanity
criminal psychology
critical thinking
the crusades
daoism
democracy
descartes
dewey
dyslexia
energy
engineering
the english civil wars
the enlightenment
epistemology
ethics
the european union
evolution
evolutionary psychology
existentialism
fair trade
feminism
forensic science
french literature
the french revolution
genetics
global terrorism
hinduism
the history of medicine
history of science
homer
humanism
huxley
international relations
iran
islamic philosophy
the islamic veil
journalism
judaism
lacan
life in the universe
literary theory
machiavelli
mafia & organized crime
magic
marx
medieval philosophy
the middle east
modern slavery
NATO
the new testament
nietzsche
nineteenth-century art
the northern ireland conflict
nutrition
oil
opera
the palestine–israeli conflict
particle physics
paul
philosophy
philosophy of mind
philosophy of religion
philosophy of science
planet earth
postmodernism
psychology
quantum physics
the qur'an
racism
reductionism
religion
renaissance art
the roman empire
the russian revolution
shakespeare
the small arms trade
sufism
the torah
the united nations
volcanoes
world war II

Beginners GUIDES

Islamic Philosophy
A Beginner's Guide

Majid Fakhry

ONEWORLD

A Oneworld Book

First published by Oneworld Publications as
Islamic Philosophy, Theology and Mysticism: A Short Introduction, 1997
Reissued 2000; reprinted 2003
First published in the *Beginners Guide* series, 2009
Reprinted 2015

Copyright © Majid Fakhry, 1997

All rights reserved
Copyright under Berne Convention
A CIP record for this title is available
from the British Library

ISBN 978–1–85168–625–4

Typeset by Jayvee, Trivandrum, India
Cover design by Simon McFadden
Printed and bound in Great Britain by Clays Ltd, St Ives plc

Oneworld Publications
10 Bloomsbury Street
London WC1B 3SR
England

Stay up to date with the latest books,
special offers, and exclusive content from
Oneworld with our monthly newsletter

Sign up on our website
www.oneworld-publications.com

Contents

Preface

The purpose of the present volume is to introduce the reader to philosophy, theology and mysticism as they developed and interacted in the Islamic context. This development over a period of almost eleven centuries may be said to have reached its zenith in the tenth and eleventh centuries, which also witnessed the most violent confrontations. However, in a serious narrative or analysis it is necessary to trace this development and interaction from beginning to end, rather than stop, as some historians of Islamic philosophy and theology have done, at the fourteenth or fifteenth century.

Throughout the discussion, I have tried to exhibit the relation of philosophy, by which theologians and mystics were influenced or against which they reacted, to its Greek and Hellenistic origins, as well as its eventual transmission across the Pyrenees to Western Europe in the twelfth and thirteenth centuries. That, I believe, is essential for demonstrating its continuity, its affiliation to the great intellectual movements in world history and its significance as an ingredient in world culture.

The reader who wishes for a more detailed discussion of the basic concepts and movements referred to in this book should consult my *History of Islamic Philosophy*, third edition, 2004 and my *Philosophy, Dogma and the Impact of Greek Thought in Islam*, 1994. I have attempted in the present volume to highlight the major philosophical, theological and mystical concepts and the problems with their interrelations in a succinct but adequate way, without bothering the reader with lengthy analyses and references. The Select Bibliography at the end of the book will give the reader a fair idea of the vast literature on the subject in Arabic and Western languages.

Finally, in transliterating Arabic proper names or technical terms, I have, with minor variations, followed the system of the *Encyclopaedia of Islam*. The translations of Qur'anic passages and other Arabic sources in this book are all mine, with very few exceptions.

Majid Fakhry
Washington DC

Introduction

The history of philosophy, which saw the light on the shores of the Eastern Mediterranean in the sixth century BCE, was marked from the start by the urge to ask the most searching questions about nature, human beings and God. That is how philosophy spawned in time the major sciences of physics, ethics, mathematics and metaphysics, which continue to be the building-blocks of world culture.

From Western Asia Minor, philosophy crossed the Aegean Sea into mainland Greece and, for a thousand years, Athens became its home. When Alexandria was founded by Alexander the Great in 332 BCE, philosophy began its eastward migration, which was virtually completed in 529 CE. In that year, the Byzantine Emperor Justinian ordered the School of Athens to be closed owing to its pagan sympathies which, as defender of the Orthodox faith, Justinian regarded as a threat to Christianity. Seven of its most illustrious teachers, led by Damascius (d. 553) and Simplicius (d. 533), made their way across the borders into Persia, where they were well received by Chosroes I (Anūshirwān), a great admirer of Greek philosophy and science. Around the year 555 he founded the School of Jundishāpūr, an important centre of Hellenic studies and medical research.

It was at Alexandria, however, rather than Jundishāpūr, that Greek philosophy was to undergo its most radical transformation. From a purely indigenous product of the Greek genius, it now became thoroughly cosmopolitan, with profound religious and mystical leanings almost unknown to the classical Greeks. Thus, the names we associate with Alexandrian or Hellenistic philosophy are those of Plotinus (d. 270), Porphyry of Tyre (d. 303) and Jamblichus (d. 330), who formulated a new brand of philosophy, designated as Neoplatonism, in which all the major currents of classical Greek philosophy, Platonism, Aristotelianism, Pythagoreanism and Stoicism were brought together in an imposing synthesis.

When Egypt was conquered by the Arabs in 641, Alexandria was still flourishing as a centre of Greek philosophy, medicine and science, as well as a Hellenized form of Christian theology which had a decisive impact on Muslim philosophy and theology, as will appear in due course. As an instance of this historic development, we note that the cultural scene began to shift eastwards, first to Damascus in the Umayyad period (661–750) and subsequently to Baghdad during the Abbāsid period (750–1258).

As the first scene of Muslim–Christian encounter, Damascus witnessed during the seventh and eighth centuries the stirrings of a new spirit of enquiry, born of political strife as well as theological controversy. In fact, the first stirrings of this spirit took a distinctly political, and often tragic, form. Because of the close correlation in Islam between the spiritual realm of religion and the temporal realm of politics, the earliest theological controversies between the Qadaris, or advocates of free will, and the traditionalists, or advocates of divine predestination, revolved around the question of political accountability. Did the Umayyad Caliphs have the right to carry out the most repressive policies or perpetrate the most heinous crimes with total impunity, since their actions were all decreed by God? Qadari theologians like Ma'bad al-Juhani (d. 699) and Ghaylān al-Dimashqi (d. 743) challenged those arbitrary claims and asserted the responsibility of the Caliphs, as well as their lowliest subjects, for their unjust deeds.

As controversy grew over questions of free will (*qadar*), divine justice and the meaning to be attached to the Divine

Speech in the Qur'an, theologians felt a growing need to turn to philosophy in general, and logic in particular, for the refinement of their concepts or methods of proof. However, a certain antipathy to Greek philosophy, because of its pagan or foreign extraction, began to surface in theological quarters. Much later, even the most skilled theologians, who had come thoroughly under the influence of Greek philosophy, such as al-Ghazāli (d. 1111), reacted violently against it on religious grounds.

Nevertheless, philosophy could boast, almost from the start, the enthusiastic support of a galaxy of distinguished scholars or authors, who assimilated and continued the legacy of their Alexandrian predecessors, with Plotinus at their head. They were fascinated by that philosopher's obsession with the concept of the unity and transcendence of the Supreme Being who generates, by an effortless process of emanation, the descending order of beings, starting with the Intellect, or Nous, and ending with the material world. The Soul, or Psyche, which emanates from the Intellect, dominates and animates the material world. After passing through a series of incarnations, it is fated to return to its original abode in the intelligible world once it has been cleansed of its earthly impurities and discovered its true identity as a citizen of that intelligible world.

What fascinated the Muslim philosophers, once they were exposed to this Neoplatonic worldview, was its profound religious and mystical pathos, especially its concept of the utter transcendence of the Supreme Being and the noble destiny it reserved for the soul in the higher world. No wonder, therefore, that the first phase in the development of Muslim philosophy was predominantly Neoplatonic. However, both in philosophical and theological circles, this brand of Greek philosophy was challenged before long and a variety of other more complex systems were proposed as substitutes. Thus al-Kindi (d. *c.*866), who still stands on the borderline between philosophy and theology, was as anxious to defend the Qur'anic worldview as he was the Greek; al-Rāzi (d. *c.*925) is far closer in outlook to Plato than to Plotinus, and others, like Ibn Rushd (d. 1198), regarded Aristotle as the paragon of wisdom or the First Teacher.

Despite their community of purpose in the pursuit or elucidation of religious truth, the philosophers and theologians (*mutakallimūn*) soon found themselves at loggerheads; the Aristotelian worldview, with its twin principles of causality and the uniformity of nature which 'does nothing in vain', as Aristotle had put it, appeared to the theologians to be inimical to the Qur'anic worldview. According to this, God can effect His designs in the world imperiously and miraculously without any impediments or restraints upon His unlimited power. Nor is He answerable for any of His actions, as the philosophers had argued in the name of divine wisdom or justice. It was for these reasons that from the tenth century the theologians adopted an 'occasionalist' metaphysics of atoms and accidents. This accorded well, they believed, with the Qur'anic concept of God's omnipotence and His sovereignty in the world, for it belonged to God alone to create or recreate the atoms and accidents which made up physical objects in the world and to cause them to cease as He pleased and when He pleased.

The pursuit of religious piety was identified from the earliest times with the strict observance of the precepts of the *Sharī'ah*, or Holy Law, as laid down in the Qur'an and the Traditions of the Prophet Muḥammad (Hadith). However, as early as the seventh century pious souls began to preach asceticism and renunciation of the world, beautifully exemplified in the lives of al-Ḥasan al-Baṣri (d. 728) and his followers, especially the great woman mystic, Rābi'ah al-'Adawiyah (d. 801). This asceticism was destined to lead in due course to Sufism, whose ultimate goal was to seek a direct channel of communication with God, either through vision or contemplation (*mukāshafah*), as al-Junayd (d. 911) and al-Ghazāli were later to claim, or through union (*ittiḥād*). This was the ultimate goal of the extravagant Sufis, such as al-Bisṭāmi (d. 875) and al-Ḥallāj (d. 922). The philosophical component in Sufism is best exhibited in the pantheistic system of Ibn 'Arabi (d. 1240) and the Ishrāqi philosophers of Persia such as al-Suhrawardi (d. 1191) and al-Shirāzi (d. 1641), who brought Neoplatonism and Sufism into harmony for the first time in Muslim history.

Following its flowering in the East during the tenth and eleventh centuries, philosophy received its major reverses at the hands of Ash'arite, Ḥanbalite and Literalist theologians and scholars. However, it soon gained a new lease of life in the western parts of the Muslim empire, al-Andalus or Arab Spain, from a galaxy of brilliant Neoplatonic and Aristotelian philosophers such as Ibn Bājjah (d. 1138) and Ibn Rushd (d. 1198). In Persia, Ishrāq marked a turning-point in the development of philosophy and Sufism and once more demonstrated the resilience of philosophy.

Prior to modern times, when philosophy was completely Europeanized, so to speak, the great moments in philosophy's history were the Greek-Hellenistic, the Arab-Islamic and the Latin-Christian. Following the fall of the Roman Empire in 476, Greek philosophy was almost completely forgotten in Western Europe, while it continued to flourish in the Muslim world. It is not sufficiently realized by most students of the history of philosophy in the Middle Ages that the 'Little Renaissance' in thirteenth century Europe was triggered by the Latin translations of the writings of al-Fārābi, al-Ghazāli (called Algazel), Ibn Sīna (Avicenna), Abū Ma'shar and Ibn Rushd (Averroes), with the consequent revival of Aristotelianism, the cornerstone of Latin scholasticism. In that respect, Arab-Muslim Spain served as the bridge across which Islamic philosophy, science and medicine crossed into Western Europe, thanks to the contribution of the great translators of the twelfth and thirteenth centuries: Gerard of Cremona, Johannes Hispanus, Dominicus Gundissalinus,

Michael the Scot, Hermannus Alemannus and others, who hailed from all the corners of the European continent.

In the East, despite reverses throughout the thirteenth and fourteenth centuries, Islamic philosophy was able to rise from its ashes. In its Ishrāqi form, it continued to be taught in the religious seminaries of Meshhed, Najaf and Qom, as well as the major universities, and it is still the subject of research and publication in Iran. In the Middle East, the teaching of philosophy was revived in Egypt by al-Afghāni (d. 1897) and Muḥammad 'Abduh (d. 1905) and continues today to be part of the educational curricula in most Middle Eastern and Arab countries, including Egypt, Syria, Lebanon, Jordan, Kuwait and Iraq. Research and publications in philosophy, whether Islamic or European, have proliferated during this century, as illustrated by the works of 'Abd al-Raḥmān Badawi, Jamil Saliba, Ibrāhīm Madkour, Zaki Nagīb Maḥmūd, Hossein Nasr and many others.

1

The transmission of ancient philosophy and science

The Greek and Syriac legacies

With the capture of Alexandria in 641, the Arab conquest of the Middle East was virtually complete. Greek culture had flourished in Egypt, Syria and Iraq since the time of Alexander the Great. The capture of Alexandria, which had become the cultural centre of the ancient world, brought the Arabs into contact with the cultures of Greece and the Middle East; for during the Ptolemaic period Alexandria had become the heiress of Athens in the fields of philosophy and science. In addition, it had become the meeting-ground of Greek speculative thought and oriental religious and mystical traditions, Egyptian, Phoenician, Persian, Jewish and Christian. The chief product of this Greek–Oriental encounter was Neoplatonism, founded by the Egyptian Plotinus (d. 270) and his most famous disciple the Syrian Porphyry of Tyre (d. 303). This brand of late Greek philosophy may best be described as a brilliant attempt to bring together the major currents in classical Greek thought, Platonic, Aristotelian, Pythagorean and Stoic, interpreted or recast in oriental religious or mystical idiom. It is not surprising, in the circumstances, that this should capture the imagination of Arab-Muslim philosophers, as illustrated by the fact that the first major philosophical text to be translated into Arabic, probably from Syriac, was a paraphrase of the last three books (IV, V and VI) of Plotinus' great work, the *Enneads*. This work was compiled by Porphyry and divided into six books of nine chapters each (hence its name, which means 'nine' in Greek). In Arabic, however, the paraphrase in question was called the *Āthulugia* (Theology) or the *Kitāb al-Rubūbiyah* (Book of Divinity) and was erroneously attributed to Aristotle by its translator, 'Abd al-Masīḥ Ibn Nā'imah of Emessa (d. 835). Although its Greek author is unknown, learned opinion today inclines to regard it as the work of Plotinus' disciple and editor, Porphyry himself.

Apart from Alexandria, centres of Greek linguistic, grammatical and theological studies flourished throughout Northern Syria and Upper Iraq well into the seventh and the eighth centuries. Of these centres, we might mention Antioch, Ḥarrān, Edessa, Qinnesrin and Nisibin, where Syriac-speaking scholars concentrated on the translation into Syriac of theological works written in Greek and emanating from Alexandria. As a propaedeutic or introductory text to the study of these works, parts of Aristotelian logic, including the *Isagoge* of Porphyry, the *Categories*, the *Hermeneutica* and the first parts of the *Analytica priora*, were translated into Syriac, excluding thereby the *Analytica posteriora*, the *Sophistica* and the *Topica*, which were deemed dangerous from a Christian point of view.

Logical and theological studies at these centres continued uninterrupted following the Arab conquest of Syria and Iraq, and produced eminent Jacobite and Nestorian scholars, such as Severus Sebokht (d. 696), Jacob of Edessa (d. 708), Georgius, known as Bishop of the Arabs (d. 774), and others.

However, translation from Syriac or Greek into Arabic appears to have started in the eighth century. The classical sources credit the Umayyad prince Khālid Ibn Yazīd (d. 704) with sponsoring the translation of medical, alchemical and astrological works into Arabic. The first accredited philosophical translations, however, are those attributed to the great literary author 'Abdullah Ibn al-Muqaffa' (d. 757) or his son Muḥammad, consisting of the *Categories*, the *Hermeneutica* and the *Analytica priora* of Aristotle, probably from Pahlavi, during the reign of the 'Abbāsid Caliph al-Manṣūr (754–73).

More important, perhaps, are the translations of Plato's *Timaeus* in Galen's synopsis or summary of that great Dialogue, Aristotle's *De anima*, the *Book of Animals*, *Analytica priora* and the apocryphal *Secrets of Secrets* (ascribed to Aristotle), undertaken by Yaḥia Ibn al-Biṭrīq (d. 815) during the reign of Hārūn al-Rashīd (786–809). However, it was Hārūn's second son, al-Ma'mūn (813–33), who placed the translation of Greek and foreign works in philosophy, science and medicine on an official footing. A brilliant and enlightened Caliph, al-Ma'mūn founded the House of Wisdom in Baghdad in 830 to serve as a library and institute of translation, headed upon its founding by Yuḥanna Ibn Māsawayh (d. 857) and shortly after by his disciple, Ḥunayn Ibn Isḥāq (d. 873), the greatest figure in the whole history of philosophical and medical translation.

Among the most important philosophical works which Ḥunayn, his son Isḥāq, his nephew Ḥubaysh and his disciple 'Isa Ibn Yaḥia, working as a team, are credited with translating were Aristotle's *Analytica posteriora*, the *Synopsis of the Ethics* by Galen, as well as the synopses of Plato's *Sophist*, *Parmenides*, *Politicus*, the *Republic* and the *Laws*. Aristotle's *Categories*, *Hermeneutica*, *Generation and Corruption*, the *Nicomachean Ethics* and parts of the *Physics*, together with the spurious *De plantis*, were translated from Syriac by Isḥāq Ibn Ḥunayn; whereas the *Metaphysics* was translated by, among others, a little-known translator, Asṭāt (Eustathius) and Yaḥia Ibn 'Adi (d. 974). Other parts of the *Physics* were translated from Greek by Qusṭa Ibn Lūqa (d. 912), who is also credited with the translation of the *Generation and*

Corruption and the pseudo-Plutarch's *Placita philosophorum*. Abū Bishr Mattā (d. 940) and his disciple, Yaḥia Ibn 'Adi, the translator of the *Metaphysics*, are credited with numerous translations, mostly from Syriac. These included the *Rhetoric* and the *Poetics* of Aristotle, which were included in the Aristotelian logical corpus known as the *Organon* in the Arabic and Syriac traditions. Al-Ḥasan Ibn Suwār (d. 1017) and Abū 'Uthmān al-Dimashqi (d. 910) are two of the better-known late translators of logical and philosophical texts.

As already mentioned, the translator of the paraphrase of Plotinus' last three *Enneads* was Ibn Nā'imah of Emessa. This paraphrase, erroneously attributed to Aristotle, laid the foundations of Arab-Islamic Neoplatonism and was commented upon by a number of Islamic philosophers, including al-Kindi, al-Fārābi and Ibn Sīna, who never questioned its Aristotelian authorship. Other pseudo-Aristotelian works translated into Arabic include the already-mentioned *De plantis* and the *Secret of Secrets*, as well as the *Book of Minerals* and the *Liber de causis*. Referred to in the Arabic sources as the *Pure Good*, the last-mentioned book was a compilation of thirty-two propositions selected from the *Elements of Theology* written by the great Neoplatonist Proclus of Athens (d. 485) and translated anonymously into Arabic prior to the tenth century. It played an important role in the development of the emanationist world-view first elaborated by al-Fārābi and his Neoplatonic successor, Ibn Sīna.[1]

The Persian and Indian legacies

The massive effort to translate the chief monuments of Greek philosophy, science and medicine into Arabic, thanks to the patronage of the early 'Abbāsid Caliphs and a cluster of other patrons, like the Barmakids, the Banū Shākir and the Banū Musa, introduced Muslims to the whole cultural heritage of the Greeks. However, Plato's *Dialogues* reached them in an abridged form, of which very few samples or excerpts have survived in Arabic. The *Politics* was the only major work of Aristotle never to be translated into Arabic. It was replaced instead by a spurious and superficial treatise purporting to have been written by Aristotle for the use of his pupil, Alexander the Great. Known as the *Secret of Secrets*, this treatise was translated by Yaḥia Ibn al-Biṭrīq (d. 815), who claimed to have discovered it in a 'Greek temple', during his travels in 'Bilād al-Rum', or Byzantium. In addition, a smattering of information about the Pre-Socratics trickled down through secondary sources such as Porphyry's lost *History of Philosophy* and pseudo-Plutarch's *Placita philosophorum*, and has been preserved in such doxographies as *al-Milal wa'l-Nihal* of al-Shahrastani (d. 1153) and the *Ṣuwān al-Ḥikmah* of al-Sijistāni (d. 1000). Of those Pre-Socratics, the names of Pythagoras and Empedocles, whose religious leanings are well known, recur constantly, but the names of Thales, Parmenides and Heraclitus are barely mentioned in the sources.

The interest of Muslim scholars in other cultures, such as the Indian and Persian, did not match their interest in Greek culture, and Roman culture remained virtually a closed book to the Arabs. Interest in Indian culture tended to turn on astronomical and medical subjects, but it is significant that the religious beliefs of the Indians were not totally ignored. Thus, Ibn al-Nadīm (d. 995), the great bibliographer, refers in his *Fihrist* to a tract 'On the Creeds and Religions of India' which was in circulation in his day and of which he saw a copy in al-Kindi's own hand. He also refers to other tracts on which he says he based his account of the religious creeds of the Indians. Our major source of information on the religious and philosophical beliefs of the Indians, however, is contained in the writings of al-Birūni (d. 1048), the great astronomer and historian, who expounded with great perspicacity, in his *Taḥqiq mā li'l-Hind min*

Maqūlah (The Truth about the Beliefs of the Indians), the fundamental beliefs of the Hindus, for which he finds apt parallels in Greek philosophy. In this book al-Birūni refers, moreover, to a little-known writer of the ninth century, Abū'l-'Abbās al-Irānshahri, who was particularly conversant with Indian religious doctrines and who appears to have influenced the great philosopher-physician Abū Bakr al-Rāzi (d. 925), especially in his concepts of space and time and the atomic composition of bodies. Some aspects of Indian atomism appear, in fact, to have been at the basis of the atomism of *Kalām*, one of the cornerstones of Islamic theology.

If we turn now to the Persian legacy, we find that it consisted primarily of the literary and moral lore of the ancient Persians. The earliest example of the literary lore is *Kalilah wa Dimnah*, or 'Fables' of the Indian sage Bidpai, translated from Pahlavi by Ibn al-Muqaffa' (d. 757). Equally important is the compilation known as *Jāwidan Khirad*, or 'Eternal Wisdom', written more than two centuries later by a fellow-Persian, Miskawayh (d. 1030), the greatest ethical philosopher of Islam. It consists, according to the author, of all that he was able to glean 'of the sermons and moral teachings of the four nations; I mean the Persians, the Indians, the Arabs and the Greeks'.[2]

The first part of this compilation consists of aphorisms and sermons of the prehistoric Persian king Ushahang (Hoshang), Buzurgimhr, Anūshirwān, Bahmān the King and others. It is noteworthy, however, that the most profound Persian influence stemmed from the religious doctrines of Manicheeism, which had an all-pervasive influence on poets, philosophers and politicians, including some Caliphs. Our sources mention, among those accused of Manicheeism, known in Arabic as *zindiqs*, or adepts of the Zend Avesta (the sacred scriptures of Zoroastrianism), the poet Bashshār Ibn Burd, Abū 'Isa al-Warrāq, members of the Barmakid family, Ibn al-Muqaffa' and the Umayyad Caliph Marwān II.

2

Early religious and political conflicts

The political scene in the seventh century

The translations discussed in chapter 1 were a major factor in the development of Muslim philosophical and theological thought. However, their impact was not felt at once and it was not until the eighth and ninth centuries that they begin to play a decisive role in theological controversies. Political conflicts, though, began to play an important role in shaping the theological outlook of rival parties as early as the seventh century.

The first serious issue to split the Muslim community following the death of the Prophet in 632 CE was the question of the legitimate successor to the caliphal office. This came to a head in the wake of the assassination of the third Caliph, 'Uthmān Ibn 'Affān, in 656. This act pitted against each other the two claimants to the caliphate, 'Ali Ibn Abī Ṭālib, son-in-law of the Prophet, and Mu'āwiyah, Governor of Damascus and kinsman of the assassinated Caliph.

According to the traditional account, as 'Ali's army was about to snatch the fruit of victory from Mu'āwiyah at the Battle of Ṣiffīn in 657, Mu'āwiyah resorted to a delaying tactic and called for arbitration. The arbitration which ensued not only confirmed Mu'āwiyah's right to the succession, but also split 'Ali's army into two rival factions, loyalists and mutineers. The mutineers, known as Khārijites or Secessionists, rejected as a grave sin (*kabīrah*) 'Ali's original consent to arbitration, in so far as it cast doubt on his rightful claim to the caliphate. From that point on, the Khārijites developed an elaborate theory of legitimacy fraught with moral and theological consequences. The Muslim community, they asserted, had the right to depose or even assassinate a Caliph deemed guilty of a grave sin, political or other. Such sin, they went on to argue, called into question the very status of the sinner as a true Muslim, who should be regarded in the circumstances as an actual infidel (*kāfir*) deserving of death. In implementation of this thesis, 'Ali was killed in 661 by a Khārijite assassin.

The Khārijites were not content to posit as a political and theological maxim the right of the Muslim community to punish the grave sinner as an apostate; they went one step further and challenged the official view, according to which the caliphal office should be confined to members of Quraysh, the Prophet's own tribe. They held instead that the members of the Muslim community, in democratic fashion, were at liberty to elect whomsoever they deemed worthy of that office, or as one authority put it, 'whoever [the Muslim community] elects as they see fit, and who deals with the people in accordance with the precepts of justice and injustice is the rightful Imam [or Caliph]. Should he change his ways and depart from the right path, he should be deposed or killed.'[1] They further allowed that the community could dispense with the caliphal office altogether, 'but if he is needed, it is lawful, whether he is a slave or a freeman, a Nabataean or a Qurashite'[2] regardless.

The Shī'ite or 'Alid party was quick to reject these claims and to pledge its unconditional allegiance to the 'Alid branch of Quraysh, asserting as their grand political maxim, in diametrical opposition to the Khārijites, that the caliphal office, or Imamate in Shī'ite parlance, was divine or necessary, so that 'the earth can never be without an Imam', as they put it. This Imam, for the Shī'ites, was not only the political head of the community, but its infallible teacher as well. Otherwise, the purity of religious truth would be jeopardized and the world would be plunged into anarchy and chaos. In the absence of a 'visible Imam', Shī'ite doctrine has stipulated from the earliest times that he is in 'temporary concealment' (*qhaybah*) and that he will appear at the end of time to fill the earth with justice, as it had been filled with falsehood and injustice.

With respect to orthodoxy or right belief (*imān*) and the status of the Muslim who commits a grave sin, which the Khārijites had raised in such a dramatic way, the Shī'ites rejected the Khārijites' ambiguous appeal to the Book of God, proclaimed at the Battle of Ṣiffīn, as well as the Sunnite or official view that the consensus (*ijmā'*) of the Muslim community was, next to the Qur'an and the the Traditions of the Prophet (Hadith), the ultimate warrant of religious and moral truth. For the Shī'ites, this warrant is the teaching of the Imam, the only infallible interpreter of the 'hidden' meaning of the sacred texts. Of the three subdivisions of the Shī'ah, the Imamites or Twelvers, the Zaydites and the Ismā'ilis or Seveners, it is the latter, followers of the Seventh Shī'ite Imam, Ismā'il, son of Ja'far al-Ṣādiq (d. 860), who pushed to its logical extreme this notion of the 'hidden truth' (*bāṭin*) of sacred texts. For that reason they are often referred to as Bāṭinis or Occultists, usually by their enemies.

The other important group which challenged the Khārijites' rigid definition of orthodoxy was the Murji'ites, who defined 'right belief' (*imān*) as 'the knowledge of God, submission to Him, abandoning arrogant defiance of Him and cordial love of Him', adding that no act of disobedience or sin could negate right belief, nor any act of obedience profit an infidel. For right belief was entirely a matter of 'inner assent', rather than external performance or practice. Should a true believer commit an act of disobedience or sin, whether menial or grave (*kabīrah*), that would not negate his right belief or his right to enter Paradise, for 'the true believer is admitted to Paradise by virtue of his sincerity and love, rather than his action or obedience'.[3]

The rise of systematic theology (*Kalām*)

The political conflicts of the seventh century had obvious theological implications, driving the warring parties to reinforce their rival positions by recourse to arguments which stemmed from what may be called common sense and the general maxims of reason. The Qur'an had allowed for such recourse in a famous passage (3, 5–6) which describes the Qur'an itself as a 'truthful revelation', confirming all previous revelations; then goes on to add: 'It is He who has revealed the Book [i.e. the Qur'an] to you [i.e. the Prophet]. Some of its verses are sound and are the Mother of the Book, and some are ambiguous (*mutashābihāt*).' The door was thus flung open for the possibility of endless conflicting interpretations (singular, *ta'wīl*), giving rise in due course to endless sectarian or factional rifts. The number of such factions is given, on the authority of an alleged Prophetic tradition, as seventy-three, only one of which is assured of salvation.

Apart from those rifts which grew out of political conflicts, the seventh century witnessed the rise of a new and revolutionary spirit, sparked off by the enquiries of the Qadaris of Damascus and Basrah such as Ma'bad al-Juhani (d. 699) and Ghaylān al-Dimashqi (d. 743), and headed by the great venerable divine and ascetic, al-Ḥasan al-Baṣri (d. 728). The speculation of those scholars turned on the question of *qadar*, or the ability of individuals as free agents to carry out their designs in the world and, *ipso facto*, to be held responsible for their actions. The official view, favoured by the Umayyad Caliphs, had been that all actions, including the Caliphs', were predestined by God. Accordingly, they could not be held responsible for them, however unjust or vile they were. Asked once what he thought of 'those kings [i.e. the Umayyad Caliphs] who spill the blood of Muslims, appropriate their possessions, do what they please and say: "Our actions are indeed part of God's fore-ordination (*qadar*)"', al-Baṣri is said to have replied: 'The enemies of God are lying?'[4] In an epistle addressed to the Umayyad Caliph 'Abd al-Malik (685–705), al-Baṣri is vehement in his censure of those kings or rulers who impute the responsibility for their evil actions to God, 'who is no unjust dealer with His servants' (Qur'an 3, 182 *et passim*). He also rejects the claims of the advocates of predestination simply to be following in the footsteps of the 'pious ancestors', who acted in conformity with God's ordinances and did not diverge from the Prophet's Way (*Sunnah*).[5]

What fuelled the controversy over the question of *qadar*, in addition to its political implications and the incrimination of the Umayyad Caliphs it entailed, was the charge that its adherents were influenced by Greek philosophy or Christian theology. We shall refer later to the role Greek philosophy played in the development of *Kalām*, but should note at this point the impact of contacts with Christian theologians at Damascus and elsewhere on the early discussions of free will and predestination. A tract attributed to Theodore Abū Qurrah (d. 826), Bishop of Ḥarrān and disciple of the great theologian of the Eastern Church St John of Damascus (d. 748), reports a debate between a Muslim (Saracen) and a Christian and the arguments levelled by the latter at the advocates of predestination, or Muslims.[6] The Arabic sources also refer to discussions between Ma'bad al-Juhani, who unleashed the whole Qadari movement, as we have seen, and Sawsan, a Christian scholar from Iraq.

By the middle of the eighth century, the Qadari movement received fresh impetus from the Mu'tazilite successor movement. Wāṣil Ibn 'Atā' (d. 748), generally regarded as the founder of this movement, was a disciple of al-Ḥasan al-Baṣri, but broke with him, we are told, over the question of the 'grave sinner'. The Khārijites, as we have seen, had maintained that such a sinner should be regarded as an infidel, whereas the Murji'ītes held that his status should be deferred (*urji'a*, hence their name), pending God's determination at the end of time. For Wāṣil, however, such a sinner should be regarded neither as a Muslim in the full sense, nor as an infidel in the full sense, but instead as lying in an 'intermediate position' between genuine belief and genuine infidelity.

Central to this type of ethical hair-splitting was the total endorsement of the Qadari libertarian position which became the Mu'tazilite hallmark. Accordingly, Wāṣil and his followers soon found themselves at loggerheads with Jahm Ibn Ṣafwān (d. 745) and his followers, who subscribed to the antithetical position of *jabr*, or strict predestination. Thus, Jahm repudiated categorically the concept of 'created power', or human ability to carry out their designs in the world, and attributed power in every shape or form to God. God, the Creator, could not be spoken of in any terms in which the creature is spoken of, such as doing, creating, being capable, causing life or death; such speech would amount to anthropomorphism (*tashbīh*). Actions, he went on to argue, were attributed to humans figuratively, in the same way that they were attributed to inanimate objects. Thus we say: 'The tree bore fruit, the water flowed, the stone moved and the sun rose and set',[7] without any implication of free will or choice. The same is true of humans, whose actions are thoroughly determined by God, just as are the punishments or rewards alleged to attach to them.

The five fundamental principles of the Mu'tazilah

The conflict between Jahm and Wāṣil tended to sharpen the point of the controversy, splitting the theological ranks into two diametrically opposed camps, the advocates of free will or *qadar* and the advocates of predestination or *jabr*. Almost all subsequent theological developments would take the form of variations on, or a synthesis of, these two antithetical positions. It is important, however, to understand fully what the Mu'tazilite movement, the first articulate theological movement in Islam, actually stood for *in toto*. Our sources report that the two grand theses around which Mu'tazilite theology turned were divine justice and divine unity, so much so that the Mu'tazilah are often referred to in these sources as the People of Justice and Unity. However, an early Mu'tazilite author, Abū'l-Ḥusayn al-Khayyāṭ (ninth century), lists five fundamental principles (*uṣūl*) on which, despite their divergences, all Mu'tazilite factions were in agreement. These are God's justice and unity, the intermediate position, God's immutable threats and rewards, His commanding the right and His prohibiting the wrong.

With respect to God's justice, the Mu'tazilah, starting with Wāṣil, inveighed vehemently against the Determinists such as Jahm Ibn Ṣafwān, because they made a mockery of the whole concept of religious obligation (*talkīf*) and rendered the concept of divine justice, affirmed in numerous verses of the Qur'an, entirely meaningless. Moreover, reason stipulates that God cannot be an evil-doer and that in holding out the promise of reward and the threat of punishment, God graciously recognizes humankind's ability to discriminate between right and wrong, through the natural light of reason, even prior to the 'advent of revelation' (*sam'*). In support of this thesis, the Mu'tazilah held that right and wrong were intrinsic qualities of human actions which were intuitively known to be either commendable or reprehensible, praiseworthy or blameworthy. God, by virtue of His wisdom and justice, they went on to argue, could only command what was right or commendable (*ma'ruf*) and prohibit what was reprehensible (*munkar*). In addition, as a merciful God, He must have regard for the welfare of His creatures, or else He would not only be unjust, but also frivolous (*safīh*). The Determinists (Jabrites or Mujbirah), and as we shall see later, the Ash'arites, took the antithetical view that God is under no compulsion of any kind, so that whatever He commands is by definition right and what He prohibits, wrong.

As for punishment and reward, the Mu'tazilah held that God would punish or reward people in the Hereafter according to the merits and demerits of their actions; some He would consign to Hell forever, as He had warned in the Qur'an, some He would consign to Paradise eternally, as He had promised. God's threats and promises being truthful, His punishments and rewards were accordingly irreversible and everlasting. In this respect, the Mu'tazilah appear to have intended to counter the view of Jahm and his followers that Heaven and Hell would perish at the end of time and nothing would remain except God's Face, as the Qur'an puts it in Sūrah 55, 27. It is not surprising in the circumstances that the Mu'tazilah should have rejected the concept of intercession (*shafā'ah*) altogether.

If it is asked now what, since humans are able to apprehend right and wrong intuitively, revelation adds to the substance of this apprehension, the Mu'tazilite answer was straightforward. Revelation, as embodied in the Qur'an, simply confirms people's moral insights, so to speak, and guards them against error. More specifically, such revelation spells out in detail the kind of moral and religious obligations incumbent upon individuals, and its ordinances are, in fact, divine 'graces' dispensed to humanity 'so that those who perish may perish knowingly, and those who live might live knowingly' (Qur'an 8, 42).

To rationalize the way in which individuals, as free agents, could carry out their designs effectively, some Mu'tazilite theologians, following the lead of Abū'l-Hudhayl (d. 841), head of the School of Basrah, resorted to a philosophical notion called generation (*tawallud*), or the causal nexus between the individual as the agent and the freely chosen action as the effect.

However, they distinguished between those actions of which the individual knows the modality, such as releasing an arrow or causing a sound to be emitted upon the collision of two hard objects, and those whose modality is not known, such as pleasure and pain, hunger and satiety, knowledge and ignorance. The individual, according to this Mu'tazilite group, is rightly designated as the author of the first type of actions, but not the second, of which God is the real author. Bishr Ibn al-Mu'tamir (d. 825) and the other Mu'tazilites of the rival School of Baghdad rejected this distinction and argued that individuals were the authors of all the actions they 'generated', regardless of whether or not they knew their modality.

Despite this and other philosophical divergences, the two Mu'tazilite branches of Basrah and Baghdad were in agreement on two fundamental principles which are essential ingredients of any genuine moral theory: namely, that in the domain of *willing*, individuals are free or capable of choice, and in the domain of outward action or *doing* (*fi'l*), they are capable of carrying out their freely chosen designs. On both scores, those theologians were at loggerheads with their Determinist rivals, who referred both the power to choose and to act exclusively to God.

An interesting variation on the theme of 'generation' was proposed by one of the most skilful Mu'tazilite theologians, Ibrāhīm al-Naẓẓām (d. 845). He advanced the theory of nature (*tab'*) according to which actions, like all natural occurrences, were forms of motion, and every such motion or occurrence was caused by God through a 'necessity of nature'. For God, according to al-Naẓẓām, has created all things initially together, and imparted to them certain specific powers or faculties, latent in other powers or faculties until such time as they are ready to become manifested in human actions or physical occurrences. This theory of latency and manifestation (*ẓuhūr wa kumūn*) appears to have been a subtle way of safeguarding the double notion of human freedom and natural efficacy without infringing God's prerogative as the ultimate or primary Agent in the universe. However, some Mu'tazilite theologians, such as Mu'ammar Ibn 'Abbād (d. 834), refined further upon the theory of nature. They argued that God was the Author or Cause of bodies only, the accidents inhering therein being the products of bodies, either naturally, as in the case of fire, which was the cause of burning, or voluntarily, as in the case of human beings who were the cause of knowledge, willing, hate and representation.

In formulating those theories of generation or causation, the aim of those Mu'tazilite scholars was clearly to counter the Determinists' claim that, as the Ash'arites generally and al-Ghazāli in particular were later to put it, nothing happens in the universe without God's direct intervention, since He is the Sole Agent in the universe. In assigning to human or natural agents a certain part in the direction or unfolding of events in the world, the Mu'tazilah were anxious in part to relieve God of the responsibility for evil in the world and thereby to safeguard His justice.

As regards the other grand theme of divine unity (*tawḥīd*), the Mu'tazilah agreed with their Jahmite rivals that God's attributes were inseparable from His essence (*dhāt*) – a thesis which the so-called Attributists challenged, contending that God possessed a series of eternal attributes, which were distinct from His essence. This thesis was regarded by the Mu'tazilite theologians generally as tantamount to a 'plurality of eternal entities'; namely God and His essential attributes, usually given as seven, including knowledge, power, life and will. They maintained, instead, as Abū'l-Hudhayl actually put it, that in God essence and attribute were inseparable and that, in fact, God was spoken of as powerful through the power which is simply Himself, and as knowing through the knowledge which is Himself, and so on. Their opponents accused the Mu'tazilah, however, of denying the attributes of God altogether; whereas their intent in insisting on the identity of essence and attribute in God was to safeguard His unqualified unity, which is such a fundamental Qur'anic tenet. In some respects, the Mu'tazilite position was also closer to that of the philosophers, who, like Aristotle and Plotinus, stressed the unqualified unity and simplicity of God, designated by Plotinus 'the One', and by Aristotle 'the Unmoved Mover' who is described as the actuality of thought thinking itself.

The attributes of God were divided by the Mu'tazilah and their rivals into *essential*, including knowledge, life, power, hearing and sight, and *active*, including will, speech and justice, all of which, according to the Mu'tazilah, were inseparable from God's essence. The first group of attributes did not, on the whole, raise any serious difficulties. When it came to rationalizing the second or active group of divine attributes and their relation to God, though, they ran into insuperable hurdles, especially regarding the two attributes of will and speech. These two attributes, which clearly bear on the mutable panorama of created objects or accidents, posed a serious threat to God's unquestioned immutability.

Take the attribute of divine will first. Abū'l-Hudhayl, the oft-mentioned head of the Mu'tazilite School of Basrah, proposed as a solution to this problem the view that the divine will was a contingent accident which inhered in no substratum, unlike the generality of accidents which always inhere in some substratum or other. In fact it was reducible simply to God's command expressed in the Qur'an in the form of the imperative: Be (Qur'an 3, 46; 16, 40, etc.), whereupon the world as the object of this command (*amr*) comes at once to be. Other Mu'tazilites, such as Bishr Ibn al-Mu'tamir, head of the rival School of Baghdad, found it necessary to distinguish between two aspects of the divine will, essential and active. The former, he argued, inheres in God's essence, whereas the latter is simply the act of creating the willed object. Other Mu'tazilite theologians, such as al-Naẓẓām and al-Ka'bi (d. 931), found the concept of will so baffling that they denied that it was predicable of God and maintained that the statement 'God has willed an object' simply meant that He had created it; whereas the statement 'God has willed the actions of human agents' simply meant that He had commanded them. God's will, in other words, is synonymous, according to those theologians, with God's creative power or command.

The attribute of divine speech (*kalām*) presented them with the same cluster of difficulties. Divine speech, manifested in divine utterances, they argued, was a created accident, and could not for that reason be regarded as eternal. However, some Mu'tazilite theologians, such as Abū'l-Hudhayl, distinguished between two aspects of divine speech: the primordial creative command through which God created the world by ordering it to be, as stated in Qur'an 3, 42; 16, 42 and 36, 82; and a secondary aspect through which God commands or prohibits certain actions. The former he declared to be an accident, which neither inheres in God (who is not a bearer of accidents) nor in the world, since prior to this command it had not come into being. The secondary aspect, according to Abū'l-Hudhayl, inheres in the particular commands or prohibitions corresponding to the primordial creative command.

At the political level, the problem of divine speech took an acute form when the 'Abbāsid Caliph al-Ma'mūn proclaimed the Mu'tazilite thesis of the created Qur'an, the prototype of divine speech, as the official policy of the state. He proceeded to implement this policy by setting up the famous Miḥnah, or Inquisition, in 827 and 833. Any religious judge (*qadi*) who refused to profess the thesis of the created Qur'an was dismissed or thrown into gaol. The most notorious opponent of this thesis at that time was Aḥmad Ibn Ḥanbal (d. 855), the leading Traditionist and scholar of Baghdad, who was unwavering in his conviction that the Qur'an, as the embodiment of divine speech (*kalām Allāh*) was uncreated and eternal. Thrown into gaol and subjected to public scourging, Ibn Ḥanbal remained adamant in his opposition to the Muʿtazilite thesis of the created Qur'an, despite all attempts at conciliation undertaken by intermediaries.

Muʿtazilite theological ascendancy continued during the reign of al-Ma'mūn and his two immediate successors; but with the accession of al-Mutawakkil in 847, the official policy of the state was completely reversed. Ibn Ḥanbal was released from prison and amends made to him; a new policy of repression aimed at the Muʿtazilah, the Shīʿah and others was inaugurated. From that time on, the star of the Muʿtazilah began to set. The theological arena was now seized by traditionalists of every stripe, until a somewhat moderate post-Muʿtazilite school led by Abū'l-Ḥasan al-Ashʿari (d. 935) appeared on the scene. In a sense, this school was destined to salvage the spirit of rational enquiry unleashed by the Muʿtazilah, despite the fact that on substantive issues the Ashʿarite school remained committed to the traditionalist viewpoint.[8]

3

The dawn of systematic philosophy and free thought in the ninth century

Al-Kindi

The history of systematic philosophical writing in Islam begins, for all practical purposes, in the first part of the ninth century. Philosophical activity heretofore consisted, as we have seen, of translations from Greek or Syriac, as well as peripheral incursions into the field of philosophical composition by some of the greater translators such as Ḥunayn Ibn Isḥāq and Qusṭa Ibn Lūqa, to whom a number of philosophical tracts are attributed, some of which have survived in Arabic.

The author who inaugurated the whole tradition of genuine philosophical writing was Abū Yūsuf Ya'qūb al-Kindi (d. *c.* 866). This philosopher, who claimed descent from the famous central Arabian tribe of Kindah, was born in Kūfah, where his father was governor of the city. Eventually he moved to Baghdad, capital of the 'Abbāsid caliphate and centre of learning and scholarship during that period. There, he enjoyed the patronage of three 'Abbāsid Caliphs, al-Ma'mūn, al-Mu'tasim and al-Wāthiq, who lent their full support to the cause of learning, scientific, philosophical and literary, and, as we have seen, identified themselves with the theological rationalism of the Mu'tazilah. When al-Mutawakkil ascended the caliphal throne in 847, al-Kindi met the same fate as philosophers and Mu'tazilites at the hands of that Caliph, but he survived al-Mutawakkil by five years. He died around 866.

Despite the scant biographical information about al-Kindi, the classical sources have preserved a large amount of information about his philosophical and scientific output. Ibn al-Nadīm (d. 995), our most reliable bibliographer, attributes to al-Kindi a total of 242 works in the fields of logic, metaphysics, arithmetic, the study of the spheres, music, astrology, geometry, medicine, politics and other subjects. This list, which has been increased by modern researchers, illustrates the vast scope of al-Kindi's learning, which was not confined to Greek philosophy, but encompassed Indian, Chaldean and Ḥarrānean religious studies, as reported by Ibn al-Nadīm. Of this vast output, only a small number of treatises, which are sometimes incomplete, have survived in Arabic or Latin-translations.

Apart from their subject matter, al-Kindi's extant writings illustrate his profound commitment to the cause of philosophy and rational discourse at a time when philosophy and the so-called 'ancient sciences' were viewed with suspicion by the traditionalist theologians and the masses at large. Among the most interesting works attributed to him is a lost tract, of which some fragments have survived, entitled *al-Haththʻala Ta'allum al-Falsafah* (Exhortation to Study Philosophy), which belongs to that age-old series of treatises exemplified by Aristotle's and Jamblichus' *Protrepticus* and Cicero's *Hortensius*. Some of his arguments in that lost tract may be reconstructed from his extant *Fi'l Falsafah al-Ūla* (On First Philosophy), in which he begins by sounding the praise of philosophy, 'the highest and noblest of human arts (*ṣinā'āt*)'. He then goes on to define it as 'the knowledge of the reality of things, according to the measure of human capacity', the highest part of which is, he says, first philosophy. This he defines as 'the knowledge of the First, True One, who is the cause of every truth'.[1] Upon this premise, al-Kindi proceeds to sound the praise of the ancients, who 'paved the way of truth for us, by exhorting us to share in the fruits of their reasons and rendered more accessible to us the hidden subjects of truth, by providing us with those premises which have paved for us the paths of truth'. Accordingly, as he had no doubt done in his lost *Exhortation to Study Philosophy*, he urges the reader to seek the truth from 'whatever source it has [emanated], even if it should emanate from races distant from us and nations different from us. For nothing is more fitting for the seeker of truth than [the pursuit] of truth itself.' This seeker, al-Kindi goes on to argue, should not be deterred by the false claims of dissimulators who bar people from the pursuit of truth in the name of religion, 'of which they are actually devoid'. Their only aim is 'to safeguard their false positions which they have earned without merit, simply for the sake of high office and trafficking with religion'.[2]

One of the arguments used by al-Kindi in his exhortation to study philosophy is a paraphrase of Aristotle's celebrated argument in his lost *Protrepticus*. As al-Kindi puts it, the study of philosophy is either necessary or unnecessary. If necessary, then we have no choice but to study it; if unnecessary, then we have to justify this claim and demonstrate its validity. Justification and demonstration, however, are part of the function of philosophy, from the study of which there is then no escape.[3]

It is significant that, despite his dependence on Aristotle, al-Kindi did not confine the function of philosophy to purely abstract thought; instead, as a good Muslim, he believed philosophy to be the 'handmaid' of religion. For the truth the philosophers seek is not different from the truth to which the prophets have summoned humankind. In fact, for al-Kindi the truth, 'to which Muḥammad the truthful, may God's blessings be upon him, has summoned, added to what he has received from God Almighty', is such that it can be demonstrated by recourse to rational arguments which only the fool can question. According to al-Kindi, to understand the intent of the Prophet in the Qur'an, it is necessary to resort to interpretation, or the pondering of the ambiguous passages of the Qur'an, in the manner of 'people of sound religion and intelligence'. He illustrates such interpretation by quoting Qur'an 55, 6 which reads: 'And the stars and trees prostrate themselves [to God]', to show how, properly interpreted, this verse describes how everything, including the outermost sphere, submits to God.[4]

From this and other examples, it appears clear that al-Kindi was one of the earliest advocates of the method of interpretation (*ta'wīl*) applied to those passages of the Qur'an specifically recognized as ambiguous (*mutashābihāt*) in Sūrah 3, 5–6. Among his contemporaries, it is clear that the Mu'tazilah and the philosophers, almost without exception, approved of the use of this method; whereas the Malikites, the Ḥanbalites and the Literalists generally did not. They clung to the explicit connotation of the sacred texts, and contented themselves, as Qur'anic commentators tended to do, with the linguistic, grammatical and rhetorical canons of reading or interpreting those texts. Their position is best illustrated by Mālik Ibn Anas' response, upon being asked about those verses of the Qur'an that speak of God 'sitting upon the Throne'. The answer of this famous jurist of Madinah, who died in 795, was straightforward, we are told by later authorities: 'The sitting is well-known, its modality is unknown, believing in it is a religious obligation and questioning it is a heresy (*bid'ah*).'[5]

The titles of many of al-Kindi's lost works, such as *Fi'l-Radd 'ala'l-Manāniyah* (Refutation of Manichaeans) and *Naqḍ Masa'il al-Mulhidin* (Rebuttal of the Propositions of Atheists), clearly reflect his Mu'tazilite sympathies. These were favourite themes of Mu'tazilite polemics. To them may be added al-Kindi's writings on divine justice, human capacity (*istiṭā'ah*) and divine unity, which were, as we have seen in a previous chapter, pivotal themes in Mu'tazilite theology and ethical theory.

In the more philosophical field, al-Kindi follows Plato's lead in re-commending the study of mathematics as a propaedeutic to the study of the higher branches of philosophy, including physics and metaphysics, or 'first philosophy', as he usually calls it. The former he defines as the study of perceptible, material and movable entities; the latter as the study of the immovable and immaterial, a definition which corresponds substantially to the Aristotelian definition of those two sciences. Beyond those two sciences, al-Kindi maintains that there is a higher 'divine science' which is acquired without human effort or discourse, but rather through self-purification and divine assistance, in a manner similar to that in which God has favoured the prophets to whom He has revealed certain truths well above or beyond the natural aptitudes of the human mind. To illustrate this higher or supernatural type of divine science, al-Kindi refers to the response of the Prophet when he was asked by the polytheists: 'Who shall revive the bones after they have withered?' (Qur'an 36, 78). He replied: 'Say, He who has created them the first time shall revive them' (36, 79). In like manner, al-Kindi argues, the verse following, which speaks of God 'providing you out of green trees with fire out of which you can light up' (36, 82), clearly and concisely illustrates God's power to produce from matter its opposite, in a manner to which human intelligence cannot aspire.[6]

For al-Kindi, the principal topic with which the science of metaphysics deals is the True One, who is eternal and infinite and, as such, has no genus or species, is not susceptible of generation and corruption and is entirely immovable. Such a Being cannot be identified with body, since the existence of an infinite body is impossible, nor can it exist in time or be subject to motion, since time and motion are specific properties of physical objects.

Of the essential properties of the One, al-Kindi highlights absolute unity, whereby He is the cause of all those entities that possess the property of unity in themselves. Hence, although multiple, they possess existence to the extent that they derive unity from the One. For 'without unity, they would not exist; their unity being identical with their existence. It is by reason of unity, then, that everything comes to be, and the True One is the Creator and Preserver of everything He has created. Were He to withhold His preservation and power, every thing would perish.'[7]

Upon these distinctly Plotinian premises, which he doubtless derived from the apocryphal *Theology of Aristotle*, on which he is is said to have written a commentary, al-Kindi bases his thesis that the One is the originator of everything, not in the manner of emanation adumbrated by the writer of the *Theology* but rather in the manner of creation *ex nihilo* laid down in the Qur'an. 'For this is the nature of primary operation (*fi'l*)', or bringing things out of nothing, which ought to be predicated of God alone. This primary operation or creation takes place *ab initio* rather than in time. Accordingly, al-Kindi advances a series of logical and mathematical arguments purporting to prove, contrary to both Aristotle and Plotinus, that time and motion are finite and the world, as the product of God's creative power, must have a temporal beginning and end. Upon this temporality (*ḥudūth*), al-Kindi then proceeds to base his argument for the existence of God. This argument, known as the argument from the temporality of the world, became in time the favourite argument of the *mutakallimun* and is stated by al-Kindi as follows: 'It is impossible that the body of the universe be eternal. Therefore this body is created in time (*muḥdath*) necessarily. Now that which is created in time must be produced by the creator in time (*muhdith*) ... The universe, then, must of necessity have a creator in time and *ex nihilo*.'[8]

Next, al-Kindi turns to the consideration of the 'proximate cause' of generation and corruption, which he regards as one of the four original Aristotelian forms of motion, i.e. locomotion; increase and decrease; alteration; and finally generation and corruption.[9] The ultimate or First Cause of generation or corruption for al-Kindi was, as we have just seen, the True One or the Cause of Causes; the proximate cause, on the other hand, is the outermost sphere, or, as he sometimes calls it, simply the heavenly body.

The first characteristic of this heavenly body or outermost sphere, according to al-Kindi, is that it lies outside the world of generation and corruption, although it imparts to that world the property of 'essential motion', which is a concomitant of life. As such, the outermost sphere must be the cause of life in the lower world and accordingly must possess life, or else it cannot impart it to lower entities. Next, being alive, this sphere or heavenly body must possess motion and perception. Some of the different forms of perception, such as smell, touch and taste, observes al-Kindi, are essential for being; others, such as hearing and sight, are essential for well-being. Of these two forms of perception, the heavenly body must possess the two higher senses of hearing and sight only.

Further, al-Kindi infers from these premises that the heavenly bodies, like the outermost sphere, must possess the faculties of intelligence or thought to a higher degree than the denizens of the lower, or sublunary world. He advances five arguments in support of this.

First, the possession of the two higher sense-faculties of hearing and sight must be a means to the acquisition of knowledge and virtue, which are the positive fruits of intelligence, or else they would have been created in vain.

Second, the heavenly bodies, being the proximate causes of our being rational, 'as decreed by God, may His praise be great', must possess the faculty of reasoning, or else we humans, who are their effects, would be nobler or higher in status than they, which is absurd.

Third, in so far as the three faculties of the soul, i.e. the rational, the irascible and the concupiscent, belong to living entities, either for their being or their well-being, the higher rational faculty must belong to the heavenly bodies, but not the other two lower faculties, which are essential for being only.

Fourth, if we compare the circumference of the earth with that of the universe as a whole, then compare the multitude of terrestrial creatures with the whole of humankind, we will see how small is the number of rational creatures when compared with the non-rational. Now, if humans were the only rational creation, it would follow that the proportion of rational beings in the universe as a whole would be very small, which is incompatible with God's wisdom and power. That is why God has decreed that the heavenly bodies, which far surpass terrestrial creatures, whether rational or non-rational, should possess the higher faculties of intelligence and foresight, whereby they are able to manage or direct terrestrial affairs.

Fifth, as the proximate causes of our being, in accordance with God's decree, the heavenly bodies must be the causes of our being rational. Were they devoid of reason, it would be impossible for them to be the causes of our being rational.

The universal order and beauty of the whole creation, as well as the manner in which God has made humankind the epitome of that creation, led the ancient philosophers (meaning the Stoics) to describe humankind as the microcosm. This view, al-Kindi hastens to comment, is perfectly compatible with the teaching of Muḥammad.[10]

As regards the influence of heavenly bodies on terrestrial phenomena, including human affairs, al-Kindi, who served a number of Caliphs as astrologer-royal, was convinced of the validity of astrological prognostications, as the titles of a number of his lost works clearly show. He also believed that the heavenly bodies had a decisive influence on the development of human character, since they determined to some extent the humours and other psychological traits of people throughout the globe. That is why, he argued, centuries before Ibn Khaldūn (d. 1406), we find that anger and lust are more common in regions lying below the equator, whereas patience, temperance and poise are more common in regions closer to the North Pole.

In the domain of psychology, al-Kindi's thought reveals a large measure of complexity. Thus, in a summary of the views of 'Plato, Aristotle and the other philosophers', he presents an essentially Platonic and Neoplatonic theory of the soul, as a divine substance 'derived from the substance of God' by way of emanation. This soul differs radically from the body which it seeks constantly to hold in check, just as the rider seeks to hold his mount in check. When the soul departs this world, it is able to know everything in it, so that nothing will remain hidden from its grasp, as Plato had argued in the *Phaedrus* and other Dialogues.

Like Plato, too, al-Kindi subscribes to the tripartite theory of the soul, or the view that the soul consists of the rational, the irascible and concupiscent parts. Upon this theory he develops, in the manner of almost all the ethical philosophers of Islam, an ethical doctrine according to which wisdom is the virtue or excellence of the rational part, courage that of the irascible and temperance that of the concupiscent part.

Upon its separation from the body at death, the soul will dwell in the world of the spheres for a while, and then ascend to the higher intelligible world. However, not all the souls will be allowed to join that higher world at once. Some will linger in the sphere of the moon, on account of their impurities, and when they are cleansed of these impurities, will be allowed to ascend to the sphere of Saturn, then that of Mercury and the other spheres beyond it. When it has become thoroughly purified, the soul will be allowed to join the intelligible world, enjoy divine favour and grasp all manners of cognition of which it was oblivious during its earthly career. Thereupon, God will entrust to it the governance of the world and the management of its affairs that it may enjoy its new assignment fully.

Finally, in a short treatise entitled *Maqālah fi'l-'Aql* (On the Intellect), which became the prototype of subsequent treatises by al-Fārābi, Ibn Rushd and others, al-Kindi develops the theme of the intellect (*'aql*), which from the time of Aristotle and his Greek commentators, especially Alexander of Aphrodisias (d. 200), would become a recurrent theme in medieval philosophy, both Eastern and Western. In this treatise, al-Kindi distinguishes four parts of the intellect: the intellect which is always in act; the potential intellect; 'the intellect which has passed from a state of potentiality to a state of actuality' or the acquired intellect; and the 'manifest' intellect, whose function is to abstract the universal forms embedded in matter. By this, al-Kindi probably meant the Active Intellect, which imparts to the soul, when it has attained the level of the 'acquired intellect', the knowledge of the species of things.[11]

Apart from psychology, and perhaps as a sequel thereto, al-Kindi discusses the way in which the truly rational person should face the hardships and tribulations of this world, the occasions of sorrow, in a major ethical treatise, *al-Ḥīlah li-Daf' al-Aḥzān* (The Art of Dispelling Sorrows). This affection of the soul may be defined simply as the pain which ensues upon the loss of what we cherish or the inability to attain what we yearn after. Now, a moment's reflection, according to al-Kindi, would show that in this world of generation and corruption, no one can keep forever what he or she cherishes or attain all that he or she yearns for. For permanence is not a feature of this world, but of the intelligible world towards which the truly wise will turn; then they will no longer be visited by sorrow or disturbed by the vicissitudes of time and fortune. Such vicissitudes are inseparable from our condition as denizens of the world of generation and corruption. Anyone who wishes that there should be no sorrow in this world wishes the impossible; for that is to wish that the nature of the generable and corruptible become ungenerable and incorruptible. It were far better to resign oneself to one's lot and face the world without fear. For fear, including the fear of death, is entirely irrational. The wise person is justified to fear what is evil; but death, as such, is not evil; only the fear thereof is evil. In fact, to wish there be no death is to wish that there 'be no man at all, since the definition of man is the living, rational and dying [animal]'. Death is therefore the consummation of our nature; 'so that were there no death, there would be no man'.[12]

Abū Bakr al-Rāzi

As the first genuine philosopher of Islam, al-Kindi stands out as a heroic figure. His championship of the nascent cause of Greek philosophy was singular, but did not weaken in the least his profound commitment to Islam. Although a great admirer of Aristotle and Plato, he was not willing to abandon or whittle down his belief in the fundamental Islamic tenets of creation *ex nihilo*, the resurrection of the body and the universal providence of God. In these two respects, he is almost without equal in the whole history of Islamic thought. Like St Thomas Aquinas (d. 1274), al-Kindi believed that reason and faith, philosophy and religion were not irreconcilable, and that a higher 'divine wisdom', imparted to mankind through revelation, did not contradict philosophy, but rather supplemented or reinforced it.

The chief successor to al-Kindi, less than a generation later, was the Persian philosopher and physician Abū Bakr al-Rāzi (d. 925/935). As a physician, his reputation both in East and West was unmatched, but as a philosopher, his reputation was marred by not unfounded charges of heterodoxy or non-conformism. Today, we know that al-Rāzi stands out as the greatest Platonist of Islam and that his philosophical output, which is no longer extant, was massive and profound. In an autobiographical tract, he informs us that he had written no fewer than two hundred treatises on every philosophical and scientific subject, with the exception of mathematics. The treatises or fragments that have survived entitle al-Rāzi to a position of undoubted pre-eminence among Muslim philosophers. His staunch espousal of Greek philosophy, like that of his great predecessor, al-Kindi, was singular and profound.

It may be noted at this point that the intellectual impetus which al-Kindi had given to philosophy and his enthusiasm for ancient learning were bound to breed a spirit of free enquiry that had far-reaching religious and political consequences. From the ninth century Muslim intellectual history was given an entirely new dimension. Al-Kindi's best-known disciple, Aḥmad Ibn Ṭayyib al-Sarakhsi (d. 899), is a good example of the hazards of unbridled philosophical enquiry. Like his master, al-Sarakhsi was engrossed in the study of logic, astronomy and *Kalām* and, as tutor and boon-companion of the Caliph, al-Mu'taḍid (892–902), he appears to have taken unwarranted liberties and broached, in the presence of the Caliph, certain heretical themes which cost him his life. According to some accounts, he is even said to have written various works in which he accused the prophets of being charlatans.

Returning to al-Rāzi, perhaps the most radical non-conformist in the whole history of Islam, it is noteworthy that his non-conformism is itself a glaring example of the new spirit of free enquiry unleashed by the study of Greek philosophy. He was born in Rayy early in the second half of the ninth century and worked in his youth as a lute-player or money-changer, we are told, before taking up medicine, in which he excelled to such an extent that he is referred to in the ancient sources as 'the unequalled physician of Islam'. Before long he became the head of the city hospital in Merw and subsequently of that in Baghdad. It is said that he practised alchemy, in addition to medicine, and towards the end of his life developed a cataract, which he refused to have removed because, as he said, he had seen enough of the world and did not want to see any more. He died in 925 or 935.

In philosophy, as mentioned above, al-Rāzi should be regarded as the chief Platonist of Islam. The titles of some of his lost works, such as *Metaphysics According to Plato's View*, *Metaphysics According to Socrates' View*, *Commentary on the Timaeus*, and so on, clearly reveal his profound Platonic leanings. In addition, our sources attribute to him a series of logical works, a *Commentary on Aristotle's Metaphysical View* and *The Criterion of Reason*, together with an autobiographical tract entitled *al-Sīrah al-Falsafiyah* (The Philosophical Way) and an ethical treatise entitled *al-Ṭibb al-Rūḥāni* (Spiritual Physic), which are both extant.

The substance of al-Rāzi's metaphysics and ethics amply demonstrates his Platonic affiliation. At the centre of his metaphysics is the theory of the five eternal principles, the Creator, the soul, matter, space and time, which can be shown to be of distinct Platonic extraction, despite minor modifications probably derived from Ḥarrānean and Manichaean sources. This is best illustrated by his theory of the soul. Like Plato, al-Rāzi argues that the soul was originally separate from matter, but was subsequently beset by erotic passion (*'ishq*) for this co-eternal principle and strove for union with it through the assumption of a material form. However, the soul could not on its own achieve this goal; therefore the Creator (*Bāri'*) had to intervene and to create the material world so that the soul might be able to be united to matter, and thereby gratify its physical lust, if only for a while. At the same time the Creator created humankind and conferred on them, from the essence of His divinity, the gift of reason, that it might rouse their souls from slumber and remind them of their original abode in the intelligible world, through the study of philosophy. However, souls engrossed in physical pleasure will continue to circle round through reincarnation, until they discover the therapeutic function of philosophy and turn towards the intelligible world. Thereupon, the lower, material world will dissolve into the elements from which it was originally made: space, matter and time.

Al-Rāzi is not content with this romantic account of the creation of the world and the process of the soul's liberation from the bondage of the body, which is the keynote of the Socratic–Platonic view of the soul in the *Phaedo*. He seeks in addition a rational answer to the question of the creation of the world. Was the world created in time or was it the product of 'natural necessity', as the Neoplatonic emanationist thesis presupposes? he asks. If by necessity, he replies, then the Creator was under compulsion to create the world; and if in time, then He was subject to the category of time like His creation. If, on the contrary, we reply, the world was created by an act of free will, we would then be forced to ask why the Creator chose to create the world at that particular point in time and no other.

By propounding his particular theory of the five eternal principles and the drama of the soul's infatuation with matter, which forced the Creator to create the physical world as the scene of the soul's self-gratification, al-Rāzi skilfully combines Platonic and possibly Ḥarrānean or Manichaean elements and concludes that the world was created in time out of pre-existing matter, as Plato had taught. Like Plato, he posits the reincarnation of the soul as a condition of its ultimate release, through the study of philosophy, from the wheel of birth and rebirth

The means to the soul's ultimate liberation, then, is philosophy, to which the Greeks were the first to point the way; for 'the Greeks are', he writes, 'the most perspicuous nation and the most patently dedicated to the quest of wisdom'.[13] Some of his contemporaries, observes al-Rāzi, believe that wisdom consists in the acquisition of those skills that grammar, poetry and rhetoric teach; but nothing could be further from the truth, according to the philosophers. The truly wise individual, according to them, is 'he who has mastered the rules of demonstration and its canons and has advanced to the point of attaining, in the fields of mathematical, physical and metaphysical knowledge the highest degree proportionate to human capacity'.[14] What need, then, does humankind have for prophethood or divine revelation, since God initially imparted the gift of reason to them 'from the essence of His divinity'? Al-Rāzi's answer is that reason is enough to enlighten or guide humankind, and accordingly prophethood is entirely superfluous. Moreover, if we peruse religious history, we will find that prophethood, or the competing claims of diverse revelations, has been the cause of endless bloodshed and warfare between the nations favoured with divine revelation (presumably for al-Rāzi, the Arab nations) and those nations, such as the Persians, who were not so favoured.

It was obviously this part of al-Rāzi's thought, and especially his unmasked repudiation of prophethood as both superfluous and nefarious, that made him the target of attack and disparagement from such diverse quarters as the Ismā'ilis, the Ash'arites and even the Peripatetics. The latter attacked him for departing from the genuine teaching of Aristotle, the former two groups for his religious heteredoxy and naturalism.

Another noteworthy feature of al-Rāzi's philosophy, which further illustrates his Platonic sympathies, is his contribution to ethical thought. Embodied chiefly in his great ethical treatise entitled *al-Ṭibb al-Rūḥāni* or 'Spiritual Physic', this treatise purports to be the counterpart of 'the corporal physic' and aims at the healing of the soul, just as corporal physic aims at the healing of the body. Al-Rāzi bases his ethical theory on the psychology of Socrates and Plato, 'the master of the philosophers and their great chief', as al-Rāzi puts it. According to them, the soul is divisible into three parts, the rational or divine, the irascible or animal and the concupiscent or vegetative, as Galen (d. 200), the great Alexandrian physician and philosopher, expressed it in his *Ethics*. (A summary of this lost work has survived in Arabic translation.) The relationship between those three parts, according to al-Rāzi, consists in the vegetative nourishing the body, which is the instrument of the soul, and the irascible assisting the rational in curbing the concupiscent. The ultimate goal of the soul is to understand its genuine nature as an immaterial substance and to strive assiduously to rejoin the intelligible world; otherwise it will be constantly afflicted with terrible pains and anxieties.

Virtue consists, according to al-Rāzi, in curbing the irascible and concupiscent soul's propensity to seek pleasure, which he defines, following Plato and Galen, as 'return to nature' (*Philebus* 31 and *Timaeus* 64). For pleasure is always proportionate to the pain resulting from departing from the natural condition; so that the pleasure of eating is proportionate to the pain of hunger, that of drinking to that of thirst and so on. The trouble with the hedonists is that, once they have experienced pleasure by allowing their souls to return to their original condition, they are unwilling to abandon it, becoming instead enslaved by it.

The strongest desire with which pleasure is associated, notes al-Rāzi, is that of sexual or erotic love (*'ishq*), which, once it has taken hold of the soul, reduces its seeker to the status of a beast. However, whereas the beast is willing to satisfy its sexual desire from any quarter, human lovers refuse to satisfy their desire from any source except the beloved, compounding thereby their humiliation and subservience, both to desire and to its object. In addition, human lovers will put up with every hardship, including anxiety, sickness and total debility, leading sometimes to madness or neurosis (*wiswās*), unless their desire is satisfied. They do not realize that sooner or later the loss of the beloved, due to parting or death, will heighten their suffering and anxiety and that it were better for them, from the start, to hold their erotic passion in check.

For al-Rāzi, the proper therapy or healing of the soul begins with the analysis of the evil propensities to which the soul is prone and from which the moral philosopher ought to cure it. These evil propensities include arrogance, envy, anger, lying, avarice, gluttony, drunkenness, sexual lust, love of worldly glory and the fear of death. The last of these is the most nefarious, because it often reduces one to a condition of total despair or anxiety. To combat this fear, two courses are recommended by al-Rāzi. The first is to understand that upon death, the soul will enter upon a better estate than its present one, especially for those who believe in the survival of the soul after death, and the rewards which the 'veridical' Holy Law (*Sharī'ah*) has promised the virtuous. The second course is to persuade those who are gripped by the fear of death that such fear is completely irrational. To do this, al-Rāzi presents a version of Epicurus' argument in his letter to Menocoeus, that no one will experience any pain or injury after death. For pain or injury is bound up with sensation, and upon death sensation ceases altogether; so that the dead will have no cause to fear death, because they will then be past all sensation. Moreover, pleasure itself, as we have seen, is nothing but return to nature, as Plato had taught; so that one who has been freed from pain through death will be free of pleasure and its tyranny. Finally, as al-Kindi wrote in his *Art of Dispelling Sorrows*, it is self-evident that to worry at the prospect of what cannot humanly be averted is the height of folly; so that the anxiety stemming from the prospect of death which is our common human lot is a form of folly, too.

According to al-Rāzi, those who lead a virtuous life, as we have seen, have no cause to fear death, so long as they fulfil the ordinances of the 'veridical' Holy Law. Should they be assailed by doubts concerning the truth of that Law, their duty is to search for the 'veridical' Law, which they are bound to find, if they try hard enough. 'If not, which is very unlikely,' writes al-Rāzi, 'then God Almighty will excuse or forgive them; since they are not accountable for what is not in their power.'[15]

The progress of free thought

As we have seen in the cases of al-Sarakhsi and al-Rāzi, among others less well known, the rationalist current unleashed by the study of Greek philosophy and the spread of Mu'tazilite theology continued to swell in the tenth and eleventh centuries. Ibn al-Rāwandi (d. 911), originally a skilled Mu'tazilite theologian, is another instance of the continued progress of free thought, in this case in theological quarters. Probably assailed by religious doubts, Ibn al-Rāwandi was led eventually to reject the whole concept of prophethood or revelation, and to argue that reason, independently of any divine revelation, was perfectly competent to distinguish between truth and falsehood, right and wrong. Accordingly, prophethood was entirely superfluous and the literary miraculousness of the Qur'an (*i'jāz*), alleged to authenticate the claims of Muḥammad to be the Apostle of God, was rationally untenable. For it is not impossible in reason, he wrote, 'that one Arab tribe [i.e. Quraysh] should excel all other tribes in eloquence, that a group of this tribe should be more eloquent than all the rest and that finally one member of that group [i.e. Muḥammad] should surpass all the others in eloquence. However, even if we grant that he exceeds all the Arabs in eloquence, what compelling force will this have where Persians,[16] who do not understand the [Arabic] tongue are concerned, and what probative evidence can he advance?'[17]

The reference to the Persians in this passage is not without significance. Many of the free thinkers or heretics, referred to generally as *zindiqs*, or adepts of the Manichaean heresy, were Persians engaged in a religious and nationalist struggle against the

Arabs and, to some extent, against Islam, as an Arab religion. They naturally found in ancient Persian religions, including Zoroastrianism and Manicheeism, a challenge to the religion of the Arabs. The most famous such *zindiq* during the 'Abbāsid period was Ibn al-Muqaffa' (d. 757), the great literary figure to whom we have already alluded in connection with the translation of Aristotle's *Categories*, *Hermeneutica* and *Analytica priora*. Other notorious *zindiqs* included Abū 'Isa al-Warrāq (d. 909), teacher of Ibn al-Rāwandi and the famous Bashshār Ibn Burd (d. 783), who met the same tragic fate as Ibn al-Muqaffa' on the charge of zindiqism.

Abū 'Isa al-Warrāq, like Ibn al-Rāwandi, was an ex-Mu'tazilite who seems to have been even more radical than his disciple in his attack on revealed religion. In his extant tracts, *Kitāb al-Maqalāt* (Book of Contentions) and *al-Radd 'ala'l-Firaq al-Thalāthah* (Refutation of the Three Sects), he attacks Judaism as well as three Christian sects, the Jacobites, the Nestorians and the Melchites, on the ground that their doctrines of the Incarnation and the Trinity do not conform to the canons of Aristotelian logic. This attack, like that of al-Kindi half a century earlier, which was the object of Yaḥia Ibn 'Adi's rebuttal, is one of the most famous encounters between Muslim and Christian theologians of the ninth and tenth centuries.[18]

However, the greatest free-thinker in Arab literary history was Abū'l-'Alā' al-Ma'arri, a poet of exceptional literary skill and personal courage. He was born in Ma'arrah, Syria, lived in Aleppo and Baghdad and died in 1057 at the age of eighty-four. An Indian strain in al-Ma'arri's thought bred a profound pessimism, almost without precedent in Islam. He led a vegetarian life, abhorred killing even a flea and asked that the following lines of verse be inscribed on his tombstone:

> This has been my father's sin,
> But I have not sinned against anyone else.

In matters of religious belief, al-Ma'arri affected an agnostic posture; he regarded reason as man's sole worthy master and divided mankind, as he put it in another famous line of verse, into 'those who possess reason but no religion and those who possess religion but no reason'. He went so far as to dismiss all the religious creeds of his day as false or ludicrous. In the following lines, he dismisses Zoroastrianism, Judaism, Christianity and Islam as equally 'puzzling':

I marvel at Chosroes and his followers
Who wash their faces with cows' urine;
And at the Jews who speak of a God,
Who loves the splatter of blood and the smell of burnt offerings;
And at the Christians' belief in a God who is humiliated,
persecuted cruelly, but does not retaliate;
And at a people who journey from the ends of the earth,
To cast pebbles and kiss the Stone.[19]
How startling are their beliefs!
Are all men, then, unable to see the truth?

Al-Ma'arri is equally startled at the 'noisy conflict' between Muslims and Christians in neighbouring Lattakia, and he declares in obvious desperation:

Each party defends its own religion,
I wonder in vain where the truth lies!

This agnosticism was never so dramatically and eloquently expressed in Arabic verse; but it had at least one great Persian exponent, Omar al-Khayyām of Nishapur (d. 1123). A great mathematician and astronomer in his own right, al-Khayyām is also the author of one of humanity's great literary treasures, the *Rubā'iyyāt* or 'Quatrains', in which he expressed the same despair at the plight of humankind and the futility of human life that other sensitive souls, including twentieth-century existentialists, have expressed. Having 'flirted' with reason and practised astronomy, al-Khayyām tells us, he was finally driven into the arms of 'the daughter of the vine', or as the 1868 version of Edward Fitzgerald's immortal English translation expresses it:

You know, my friend, how bravely in my house,
For a new marriage I did make carouse;
Divorced old barren reason from my bed,
And took the Daughter of the Vine for spouse.

For is and is-not, though with rule and line,
And up-and-down by logic I define,
Of all that one should care to fathom, I
Was never deep in anything but wine.

Of the overpowering dominion of fate, al-Khayyām writes:

The moving finger writes and having writ,
Moves on; nor all your piety and wit
Shall lure it back to cancel half a line,
Nor all your tears wash out a word of it.

His despair, however, reaches its peak in these lines in which he says, having reached the 'Throne of Saturn', and as an astronomer, unravelled many a knot on the way, he could still not unravel the mystery of fate:

There was the door to which I found no key;
There was the veil through which I could not see;
Some little talk awhile of me and thee
There was, and then no more of thee and me.[20]

4

Neoplatonism and Neopythagoreanism in the tenth and eleventh centuries

Al-Fārābi

Al-Kindi's eclectic thought, as we have seen, was marked by certain Aristotelian leanings in metaphysics and Stoic undertones in ethics. Al-Rāzi's outlook, however, was essentially Platonic, with possible Ḥarrānean and Manichaean accretions. The first truly systematic philosopher of Islam was Muḥammad Ibn Muḥammad Ibn Ṭarkhān Ibn Uzlagh al-Fārābi, who laid down the foundations of Islamic Neoplatonism.

Little is known about al-Fārābi's life other than the fact that he was born in Fārāb in Transoxiana and that his father was a captain in the Persian army, probably of Turkish or Turkoman extraction. He is said to have arrived in Baghdad at the age of forty and studied with the leading logicians of the time, including Abū Bishr Mattā and Yuḥanna Ibn Ḥaylān. After a short trip to Egypt, he settled briefly in Aleppo at the court of the Hamdani prince Sayfal-Dawlah, a great patron of learning who showed a great deal of regard for al-Fārābi. Shortly afterwards, he moved to Damascus where he died in 950 at the age of eighty.

The three areas in which al-Fārābi excelled were logic, political philosophy and metaphysics. In logic, he wrote commentaries on, or paraphrases of, all the parts of Aristotle's logical corpus, known as the *Organon*, in addition to the *Rhetoric* and the *Poetics*, which formed part of the *Organon* in the Syriac and Arabic traditions, as well as the *Isagoge* of Porphyry. His original logical tracts dealt chiefly with the analysis of logical terms in a manner which goes well beyond the *Categories* of Aristotle and the *Isagoge* of Porphyry, and include *al-Alfāz al Musta'malah fi'l-Manṭiq* (The Terms Used in Logic), *al-Fusūl al-Khamsah* (The Five Sections on Logic) and *Risālah fi'l Manṭiq* (The Introductory Epistle), which are all extant. These tracts, as well as his other logical treatises of which a large number are no longer extant, illustrate al-Fārābi's standing in a field which had been, up to his time, almost the exclusive preserve of Syriac-speaking Christian logicians, including his two above-mentioned teachers. Those logicians, we are told, did not proceed beyond the first part of Aristotle's *Analytica priora* for theological reasons, a practice with which al-Fārābi was the first to break.

To highlight further al-Fārābi's unique standing in the history of Islamic philosophy, we may mention a group of his 'methodological' treatises, such as the *Philosophy of Plato and Aristotle* and the *Reconciliation of Plato and Aristotle.* In these, he paved the way for further study of philosophy. In his *Ihṣā'al-'Ulūm* (Enumeration of the Sciences), in particular, he first introduced his contemporaries to the Greek philosophical curriculum, or the classification of the linguistic, philosophical and other sciences of his day.

The philosophical sciences, according to al-Fārābi, include mathematics, with its many subdivisions into arithmetic, geometry, astronomy, astrology, music, mechanics and so on. Next come the natural sciences, whose subdivisions correspond to Aristotle's eight physical treatises, i.e. the *Physics*, the *Heavens*, *Generation and Corruption*, the *Meteorology*, the *Book of Minerals*, *On Plants*, the *Zoology* and *On the Soul.*[1] These are followed by the 'divine science', as metaphysics was often called in the

Arabic sources, which according to al-Fārābi is entirely embodied in the *Metaphysics* of Aristotle, also referred to in the Arabic sources as the *Book of Letters*. It has three subdivisions:

1. a part which investigates existing things, in so far as they exist, i.e. ontology;
2. a part which investigates the primary principles of demonstration, common to logic, mathematics and physics, i.e. epistemology, or the metaphysics of knowledge;
3. a part which investigates immaterial substances, their number and essence and the way in which, 'although multiple, they rise from the lowest to the higher and then the higher, until they terminate ultimately in a perfect being, nothing more perfect than which can exist'.[2]

This last point summarizes in Arabic one of the best-known proofs for the existence of God, called the ontological argument, first formulated in the Middle Ages by St Anselm (d. 1109) and restated in modern times by Descartes (d. 1650).

The three sciences which close the *Enumeration* are politics, jurisprudence (*fiqh*) and theology (*Kalām*). The first, explains al-Fārābi, deals with ethical traits and voluntary modes of conduct which determine specific actions and the purposes at which they should aim, culminating in the pursuit of happiness or well-being. Jurisprudence is then defined by al-Fārābi as the art of extracting from the explicit statements of the Lawgiver the rules governing actions and beliefs, for which explicit legislation has not been enunciated; whereas theology is defined as the art of supporting, by recourse to rational discourse, the beliefs or actions prescribed by the Lawgiver, as well as refuting contrary beliefs or actions. This, in fact, was the double function of *Kalām*, as we have seen in the case of the Mu'tazilah. Al-Fārābi was undoubtedly thinking of them in his formulation of the definition of *Kalām*.

Apart from these 'methodological' questions, the substance of al-Fārābi's philosophy is actually contained in his best-known work, *Mabādi Ārā' Ahl al-Madīnah al-Fāḍilah* (Principles of the Opinions of the Inhabitants of the Virtuous City). In this work, al-Fārābi has given a general outline of the universe at large, the mode of its emanation from the First Being and finally the virtuous mode of political association and the ultimate destiny of the soul.

The groundwork of this utopian undertaking, which is of definite Platonic inspiration, is essentially Neoplatonic in its metaphysical and cosmological aspects. Thus, the discussion opens with an account of the First Being, the Cause of all existing things, and of His essential attributes.

This Being, according to al-Fārābi, is:

1. perfect, or free from every imperfection in such a way that nothing can be prior or superior to Him;
2. eternal, or not susceptible of any privation, contingency or potentiality;
3. not liable to composition of matter or of form, since those two terms are correlative;
4. such that He has no purpose or aim other than Himself, and does not derive His being from anything other than Himself.

Such a Being, al-Fārābi goes on to argue, is utterly unique, and therefore can have no partner or associate; and being entirely separate from matter, He must be an intellect in act, since matter is the chief hindrance to intellectuality. By the same token, He should be intelligible in act; that is the object of His own intellectual activity. Accordingly, as Aristotle had expressed it in *Metaphysics* XII, 9, the very nature of this Being is thought thinking thought. As such, al-Fārābi continues, following Aristotle, the First Being must be living; for life is the act of 'apprehending the best intelligibles through the best mode of intellectual apprehension'.[3] When He apprehends Himself in this way, the First Being partakes of the greatest pleasure attendant upon the love of His own beauty and perfection, and may now be defined as love loving itself.

Next, al-Fārābi proceeds to argue in the manner of Plotinus and Proclus, the two great Neoplatonists of late antiquity, that the First, being fully perfect and self-sufficient, must, by virtue of His superabundant goodness, overflow or emanate, giving rise in that way to the whole hierarchy of existing entities. However, such an emanation (*ṣudūr*) should not be supposed to be the cause or purpose of the being of the First, who is perfect. Rather the contrary; His self-sufficient being, 'by virtue of which He exists by Himself is nothing other than the being through which the being of other things arises from Him';[4] in other words, His being and that of all other things which derive from Him by way of emanation are identical.

The emanation of subordinate entities from the First follows the principle of regression or devolution, the most perfect giving rise to the less perfect; thus the first emanation from the First is the first intellect, which apprehends both itself and its source. When it apprehends the First, it gives rise to the second intellect; whereas when it apprehends itself, it gives rise to the first heaven. In the sequel, the third intellect and the sphere of the fixed stars corresponding to it arise in succession, then the fourth intellect and its corresponding sphere, or that of Saturn. This process continues until the fifth, sixth, seventh, eighth, ninth and tenth intellects, together with their corresponding spheres, are progressively generated. With the tenth intellect, which governs the sublunary world (or the world of generation and corruption, as Aristotle called it), the series of intellects is complete and the stage is set for the rise of the generable–corruptible entities of the lower world. These entities arise through composition from matter and form, and are entirely different from the intellectual entities of the higher or intelligible world. The order of their generation is the reverse order of ascent from the lowest to the highest grade of becoming: from prime matter the four elements, then minerals, plants, animals and humans are generated in succession.

Al-Fārābi accounts for the emanation of terrestrial from celestial entities by arguing that the prime or common matter of terrestrial entities emanates from the 'common element' of heavenly bodies, by which he can only mean Aristotle's ether or the 'fifth element'. The contrary forms, or four primary qualities of Aristotelian physics, then combine with the four elements mentioned above, to give rise to the multitude of corporeal entities in the physical world.

Humankind, which marks the climax of the terrestrial process of generation and corruption, arises as a result of the last and highest combination of the simple elements and their corresponding compounds. The first human faculty to emerge as a result of this combination is the nutritive, followed by the sensitive, then the desiderative, the imaginative and finally the rational, with its three subdivisions: the theoretical, the practical and the productive.

Each of these faculties, according to al-Fārābi, has a ruler or head, a series of tributaries and subordinates. The ruler of all these faculties is the heart, which is the source of 'animal heat', the original principle of life in animate objects diffused throughout the vessels and the different organs of the body. The function of the brain is simply to 'moderate' this animal heat, so as to render it proportionate to each organ of the body. Here al-Fārābi appears to agree with Aristotle, for whom the heart was the seat of perception and thought, unlike Galen who located them in the brain. However, the brain, for al-Fārābi, has two additional functions. The first is to endow the nervous system with the power to enable the five senses, described by him as tributaries, to perceive in actuality. The second function of the brain consists in endowing the motive or muscular system with the power to move in response to the desiderative faculty, residing in the heart.

The brain is succeeded in descending order by the liver, the spleen and the genitals, each of which performs its function in an orderly manner, whereby the lower faculty is always subservient to the higher. Of interest is the way in which the five external senses subserve the principal internal senses, i.e. the *sensus communis*, the imagination and memory, which together co-ordinate the 'sensible forms' received through the five senses. In a similar manner, the 'intelligible forms' received by the rational faculty from the Active Intellect are co-ordinated by this faculty. The first such forms are the material, which the rational faculty abstracts from their material substrata through the potential intellect, assisted by an 'external agency', which is the Active Intellect. This intellect is to the preceding material intellect what light is to visible objects, and its rank in the scale of intellectual emanations, as we have seen, is the tenth.

The first group of intelligible forms apprehended by the rational faculty, assisted by the Active Intellect, are the 'common primary intelligibles', which are part of the first principles of the sciences and the arts, and are known intuitively. Al-Fārābi then divides them into three sub-groups: the first principles of geometry, the general principles of ethics and the ultimate principles of all existing entities, such as the First Being and the heavenly bodies from which existing entities derive their being through emanation.

It is noteworthy that al-Fārābi was the first Muslim philosopher to discuss in great detail the classic problem of the intellect, bequeathed to posterity by Aristotle. In a famous treatise, *Risālah fi'l 'Aql* (On the Intellect), al-Fārābi lists six different meanings of the term 'intellect' or 'reason'.

The first is the reason which the public predicates of the prudent or perceptive person, designated thereby as reasonable. Second is reason as understood by theologians when they say that reason affirms or denies such an opinion. This sense of reason is reducible, according to al-Fārābi, to 'what is concurred in by the general public or the majority'.[5] Then follows the reason which the 'Master Aristotle' has mentioned in *Analytica posteriora* (*Kitāb al-Burhān*), described as the *habitus* (*malakah*) through which the first principles of demonstration are intuitively known. The fourth meaning of reason is what is referred to in Aristotle's *Nicomachean Ethics* as 'the practical reason through which, following prolonged experience and time, the certain knowledge of propositions or premises, bearing on voluntary matters, which ought to be either chosen or shunned, is attained'.[6] Fifth is the reason discussed in *De anima*, which itself admits of four divisions:

1. potential or material reason, to which it belongs to abstract material forms from their material substrata;
2. actual reason, in which those forms reside once they have been abstracted by the potential intellect;
3. acquired reason, in which intelligible forms reside once they have been stripped of every material accretion. This reason, which is able to apprehend those intelligibles at will, may be described as the zenith of human cognitive capacity and the borderline between the material world and that of separate intelligences;
4. the Active Intellect, which is the lowest of these intelligences, and may be described as the supermundane agency which imparts to human reason the power to actualize its cognitions. It is in that respect analogous to the sun, which makes potentially visible objects actually visible.

However, unlike Aristotle, whose view he is here interpreting, al-Fārābi attributes a semi-creative role to the Active Intellect. As the immaterial agency in which the intelligible forms are stored, lying on the periphery of the sublunary world, this intellect imparts to material objects those substantial forms that constitute their very essence. It is these forms that the acquired intellect then abstracts in the highest stage of human cognition, described by al-Fārābi as 'proximity' to, or 'contact' (*ittiṣāl*) with the Active Intellect. This contact became for Muslim Neoplatonists, following the lead of al-Fārābi, the ultimate fulfilment of humankind's intellectual nature.

The sixth reason is that referred to in Aristotle's *Metaphysics*, as thought thinking itself, or God. He is, for al-Fārābi, entirely free of materiality or imperfection, and is the Cause of all the subordinate intellects, including the Active Intellect, which is not free from imperfection, since its activity is not continuous. In fact, unlike that intellect or First Reason, whose activity is uninterrupted, the Active Intellect may be barred from acting upon its objects, material or other, by some external impediment or contingency.

After completing his discussion of the rational faculty, al-Fārābi turns to the two practical faculties of will and desire. Will is defined by him as the desire for that which is apprehended by sensation or imagination and is common to humans and the higher animals, unlike choice, which depends on deliberation or thought and is exclusively human.

The ultimate goal of rational desire or choice, according to al-Fārābi, is happiness. This consists in the soul's dissociating itself from everything material or bodily and joining the host of 'separate intelligences' in the intelligible world, which, like Plato, al-Fārābi believed to be the soul's ultimate abode. However, like Aristotle, he believed the individual to be a *zoon politicon* who could not attain the ultimate goal of happiness, outside society. The 'solitary' life, later to be recommended by the Sufis and Ibn Bājjah (d. 1138), his Andalusian spiritual disciple, is repudiated by al-Fārābi, despite his espousal of the semi-mystical ideal of 'contact' with the Active Intellect that is the object of all human cognition and choice. 'Human perfection,' he writes in the *Opinions of the Inhabitants of the Virtuous*

City, 'for the sake of which human nature was ordered', is not possible without human association. Such association takes three forms: the largest, corresponding to the whole inhabited world; the intermediate, corresponding to the nation or *ummah*; and the smallest, corresponding to the city-state (*madīnah*). According to al-Fārābi, it is within the last that human perfection is best attained. The city in which human happiness is achieved through the co-operative effort of its citizens is designated by al-Fārābi as the 'virtuous city'; all other cities are simply referred to as its 'opposites'.

The first of these generic forms of human association is the ignorant city, whose subdivisions are:

1. the necessary city, whose inhabitants have never apprehended the nature of true happiness and thus are content to seek material well-being and the bare necessities of life;
2. the ignominious city, in which they are simply content to seek wealth or material possessions;
3. the city of meanness, in which pleasure is the chief goal;
4. timocracy, or the 'city of honour', in which honour or public esteem is the goal;
5. tyranny or despotism, in which conquest or domination is sought by the citizens;
6. democracy, in which individual freedom, resulting in lawlessness or anarchy, is their goal.

The second generic form of 'opposite' or corrupt city is the wayward, whose inhabitants have apprehended the truth about God and the afterlife, but have failed to live up to it. The third form is called by al-Fārābi the perverted city, the opinions of whose inhabitants were originally true and their actions virtuous, but in time became perverted or false. The fourth form is the erring city, whose inhabitants entertain false opinions about God and the Active Intellect and whose leader is a false prophet, who resorts to treacherous and deceitful means in carrying out his designs.[7]

By contrast, the virtuous city stands out as a moral and theoretical model, in so far as its inhabitants have apprehended the truth about God, the Active Intellect and the afterlife, and live according to the precepts of virtue. At its head stands a ruler, who presides over its many parts or classes in a judicious way. This ruler must be qualified by nature and nurture to assume the position of leadership and to receive the illumination of the Active Intellect in such a way that, by reason of the perfection of his theoretical and practical faculties, he will be a philosopher, and by reason of his ability to foretell the future through his contact with the Active Intellect, he will be a prophet. Al-Fārābi then goes on to enumerate in a more specific way the qualities which, like Plato's philosopher-king, his philosopher-prophet should possess, in order to qualify fully for his noble office at the head of the virtuous city. The most important of the twelve qualities he prescribes are love of justice, truthfulness, quickness to learn, soundness of body and limb, eloquence, nobility of character, temperance and courage. Many of those qualities, it will be noted, are actually identical with those of Plato's philosopher-king as given in *Republic* VI, as well as those which the Caliphs were supposed to possess according to Muslim jurists and legal scholars.

From this analysis, it will appear that al-Fārābi's virtuous city-state is really a blend of Platonic utopianism and Islamic political doctrine. In Islamic political theory, the Caliph–Imam was also expected to be guided by the ordinances of the *Sharī'ah* rooted in divine revelation. In some ways, this revelation is analogous to the illumination of the Active Intellect. Al-Fārābi was the first Muslim philosopher to extract this concept from the emanationist metaphysics and cosmology of Plotinus and Proclus, and to erect upon it a political utopia, corresponding in many respects to the caliphal model, especially in its Shī'ite or Imamate form.

Ibn Sīna

Ibn Sīna, who acknowledges explicitly in his autobiography his debt to al-Fārābi, may be said to have developed the fundamental Neoplatonic themes adumbrated by his predecessor, with the exception of politics. However, his style of writing far surpassed that of al-Fārābi in elegance and fluency, and this probably ensured for his writings a far greater diffusion in learned circles, so that his name became identified in time with Islamic Neoplatonism, although its real founder was al-Fārābi.

In his autobiography, Ibn Sīna informs us that he was born in Afshaneh, not far from Bukhara, to which he later moved with the rest of his family. In Bukhara, we are told, he studied with a number of teachers, of whom he mentions al-Nātili, Ismā'il the Ascetic, and an Indian grocer proficient in arithmetic. However, he was soon able to dispense with the services of those teachers and to turn to the study of philosophy and medicine on his own. By the age of sixteen, we are also told, he attained such a standing in medicine 'that many distinguished physicians started learning from me', seeing, as he adds, that medicine is not such a difficult subject. The only subject at which he balked was metaphysics; he read Aristotle's *Metaphysics* forty times, he says, without understanding the intent of its author, until he lighted on a treatise of al-Fārābi entitled *On the Intentions of the Metaphysics*. This treatise unlocked for him the secrets of that book, which he already knew by heart.

By the age of twenty-one, Ibn Sīna started to commit his ideas to paper. His writings, which totalled 276 according to a modern inventory, covered the whole range of philosophical, scientific, medical and even linguistic studies. They rank among the most exhaustive and systematic writings in Arabic and, to a larger extent, in Persian. Most of those writings have survived. They include *al-Shifā'* (Healing), *al-Najāt* (Salvation) and *al-Ishārāt* (Indications). To these should be added a number of mystical or Ishrāqi tracts such as *The Epistle of the Bird*, *The Epistle of Love* and *Ḥayy Ibn Yaqẓān* (Living Son of Wakeful). The most important of these writings is unquestionably *al-Shifā'*, a genuine *summa philosophica* in some fifteen volumes, covering the whole range of the philosophical sciences known in his day. *Al-Najāt* is an abridgement of this work, made by Ibn Sīna himself.

Unlike al-Fārābi, his avowed spiritual master, Ibn Sīna does not appear to have taken any serious interest in political philosophy or ethics; his contribution in these two fields is comparatively trivial. However, his interest in metaphysics and logic was profound, as illustrated by the space he devoted to those two subjects in *al-Shifā'*, *al-Nājat*, *al-Ishārāt* and elsewhere. His metaphysical outlook, like that of al-Fārābi, was Neoplatonic. The cornerstone of this Neoplatonism is the emanationist view propounded in the *Pseudo-Theology*, on which he is said, like al-Kindi, to have commented. However, in some of his writings, especially the opening parts of *al-Shifā'*, he expressed a certain disenchantment and dissatisfaction with the conventional Neoplatonism or Peripatetism (*Mashshā-'iyah*) of his day, claiming that his own views should be sought in the *Oriental Wisdom*, which embodied the 'unadulterated truth'. Ibn Sīna claims to have tapped the oriental source of this wisdom, without offering any conclusive evidence.

Whether Ibn Sīna did in fact complete the *Oriental Wisdom*, of which the logical part has reached us, is an open question. His later works such as *al-Ishārāt* and the shorter 'mystical' tracts exhibit, on the whole, a mystical strain in his thought which is not radically different from al-Fārābi's or Plotinus', and may be described as philosophical or rational mysticism. Unlike the extravagant mysticism of his predecessors such as al-Hallāj and al-Bisṭāmi, this philosophical mysticism consists in the intellectual urge of the soul to achieve contact or conjunction (*ittiṣāl*) with the Active Intellect, or conversely the divine Nous of Plotinus, rather than union (*ittiḥād*) with, or even vision (*kashf, mushahadah*) of, God, who both for Plotinus and the Muslim Neoplatonists continues to be unattainable.

In *al-Shifā'*, Ibn Sīna begins by defining metaphysics in a conventional way as the study of entities which are immaterial, both in essence and definition. It is called by some, he informs us, the divine science, which investigates the first principles of physical and mathematical entities, leading up to the Cause of all causes and the First Principle of all principles. It is for this reason called the first philosophy or absolute wisdom.

This definition, which is clearly Aristotelian, is then rejected by Ibn Sīna on the ground that the First Cause or God, alleged to be the *subject* (*mawḍū'*) of metaphysics, is actually one of the objects (*maṭlūb*) or questions it seeks to demonstrate. The proper subject of metaphysics, for him, is being *qua* being, which is intuitively known and should be posited as the starting-point of that science. In other words, the core of metaphysics, for Ibn Sīna, is ontology (the study of being *qua* being), of which the categories of quality, quantity, position, action and passion, as well 'the proper concomitants' of actuality, potentiality, necessity, universality, unity and multiplicity are so many predicates.[8]

Despite this important caveat, Ibn Sīna, like al-Fārābi and the Peripatetics in general, goes on to divide metaphysics into three parts:

1. a part dealing with the ultimate causes of existing entities in general, and God in particular;
2. a part dealing with the concomitants of being and its properties, listed above;
3. a part dealing with the first principles of knowledge common to all the sciences.

Nevertheless, the largest part of Ibn Sīna's metaphysics deals, in fact, with being, its relation to the categories and the proper concomitants, or universal concepts attached to it. The first major premise of this 'ontological' approach to metaphysics, as already mentioned, is that being or existence (*wujūd*) is a primary notion which is apprehended at once and does not depend on any other notion prior to or more knowable than it. In that respect, it is analogous to the concept of 'one' or 'thing', and like these two concepts is indefinable.

The second major premise is that the nature or essence of an entity is clearly distinguishable from its existence. Thus, if we say that the essence (*māhiyah*) of a given entity exists, whether in fact or in thought, our statement would be meaningful; but if we say that its essence is its essence, our statement would be meaningless. In other words, being or existence adds to an essence a specific determination external to it.

The third major premise is that the not-being or non-existent exists in some sense or other. Our statement that an entity is non-existent may be interpreted to mean that although non-existent in fact, it exists in thought. As for the absolutely non-existent, it is impossible to speak of it affirmatively; and when we speak of it in negative terms, it would acquire an existential status as a concept in the mind, that is as a conceptual mode of existence. This view, it will be recalled, accords with the earlier view of the Mu'tazilah that the non-existent (*ma'dūm*) is a thing (*shāy*), since it existed in God's mind prior to its creation. Ultimately, it is affiliated to the Platonic view that particulars of sense pre-existed eternally in the World of Ideas, as paradigms of objects of sense.

The discussion of essence and existence leads Ibn Sīna to introduce his famous metaphysical distinction between contingency and necessity, upon which is built his whole view of the Necessary Being, as distinct from the contingent universe. He defines the necessary in *al-Shifā'* as 'that which, conceived in itself, must necessarily exist', and in *al-Najāt*, less tautologically perhaps, as 'that being which, if it is supposed not to exist, an absurdity will ensue';[9] unlike the contingent which, whether we suppose it to exist or not, would entail no such absurdity.

Upon this distinction as a first premise, Ibn Sīna then proceeds to develop his famous proof for the existence of the Necessary Being, known up to the time of Leibniz (d. 1716) and Kant (d. 1804) as the proof from the contingency of the world, or *a contingencia mundi*. This proof begins by recognizing that being exists, and as such, it should be either necessary or contingent. If necessary, then the existence of God as the Necessary Being has been proved; if contingent or possible, then its existence must depend ultimately on the Necessary Being. For it is impossible that the series of causes upon which the existence of contingent beings depends should go on *ad infinitum*. Now, the members of this series exist either simultaneously or not; if simultaneously, then the series as a whole, whether finite or infinite, will again be necessary or contingent. If necessary, then it is impossible that every member thereof should be contingent, since it has been described as necessary. Therefore, it must include a member who is necessary and is the cause of the whole series. Such a cause must lie outside the series; otherwise it will, in fact, be contingent, like the other members of the series, and this has been shown to be impossible. If, on the other hand, the series as a whole is contingent, it will require a cause, lying outside the series, who is necessary. In either case, the series of contingent entities making up the world will depend on a Necessary Being who is its ultimate cause.[10]

Ibn Sīna does not explicitly discuss the other possibility; namely, that the members of the series of contingent entities mentioned above may not exist simultaneously but in succession, although he does consider the alternative, that such entities may exist cyclically (*dawran*) in such a way that each is the cause of the other. However, this latter alternative, like the former, is for him impossible, and the series of contingent entities must be supposed to have a cause who is necessary, no matter what the temporal status of its members may be.

Next, Ibn Sīna discusses the attributes of this Necessary Being, the foremost of which, next to necessity, is absolute unity. By this we should understand that the Necessary Being is free from every mode of multiplicity or composition, including the composition of essence and existence. For, were He supposed to be composed of essence and existence, as is the case with all generable and corruptible entities, then He would need a cause to bring His essence into existence, since essence, as such, cannot cause itself to exist. In that case, the Necessary Being would not be the First Cause, as has already been proved.

If it is the case that the Necessary Being, then, has no essence apart from His existence, with which He is identical, then He will have no genus or species and is, therefore, indefinable. In addition, He is free from quantity, quality, position or any other accidental property, and therefore has no equal or partner (*sharīk*).

It will be noticed that the above attributes are negative; therefore Ibn Sīna proceeds to supplement them with a series of positive attributes. Thus, the Necessary Being is described as the pure good, pure reason and pure truth. By pure good, we should understand the ultimate object of desire towards which all things tend, or the source of all perfection and goodness imparted to existing entities by way of emanation or bounty. By pure truth, we should understand the fact that the Necessary Being is the most truthful and everlasting being, and accordingly the most worthy of existence. As for His being pure reason or intellect (*'aql*), this follows from His being entirely free from materiality, and everything free from materiality, as al-Fārābi had also argued, should be regarded as pure reason, whose object is no other than itself. The Necessary Being is, then, thought thinking itself (*'aql, 'āqil* and *ma'qūl*).[11]

The mode of the Necessary Being's knowledge of existing entities, which was to be at the centre of the most heated controversies between the philosophers and the theologians in the centuries to come, is such, according to Ibn Sīna, that it entails no multiplicity or change in His essence, as the theologians were later to contend; because this knowledge is not dependent upon those entities in the manner of human knowledge, as their effect, but is rather their cause. 'For as the First Principle of all existence, He knows Himself as the cause (or First Principle) of that of which He is the principle', or the totality of all things whether corruptible or incorruptible.[12] It follows that He knows everything, whether in the higher world of intelligibles or in the lower world of corruptible entities, in 'a universal way'. Nevertheless, Ibn Sīna hastens to add, as though in anticipation of al-Ghazāli's objection that he had thereby robbed God of the knowledge of particulars, 'nothing particular, however, escapes His knowledge; so that not even an atom's weight in the heavens or the earth escapes Him. This, indeed, is one of the wonders whose understanding requires a subtle acumen.'[13]

If we turn now to the origination of the world, we will note that Ibn Sīna, like al-Fārābi, his spiritual master, regards the world as an emanation from the Necessary Being, who in an act of pure generosity or bounty (*jūd*) overflows (*yafīḍ*), giving rise in the first place to the first intellect, which is one, but by reason of its dependence on the Necessary Being is partly necessary, partly contingent. When this first intellect apprehends its author, it gives rise to the second intellect, but when it apprehends itself, it gives rise to the soul of the outermost sphere or its body, depending on whether it apprehends itself as necessary in relation to the Necessary Being, or contingent in itself. The process of emanation, then, continues whereby the series of intellects and their corresponding spheres are generated, until the tenth or Active Intellect, which governs the sublunary world, is finally generated. Thereupon, the world of the elements comes into being, wherein the simple elements combine with the 'substantive forms' emanating from the Active Intellect to give rise to the multitude of particular entities making up that world.

The Active Intellect, which is an intermediary between the intelligible and the material worlds, thus plays a fundamental 'cosmic' role. It imparts the above-mentioned 'substantial forms' to the elements or their compounds once they have become 'disposed' for their reception. In addition, it plays an equally fundamental 'cognitive' role, in so far as it is the storehouse or 'locus' of all intelligibles, imparting to the human mind those primary intelligibles or forms that constitute the very stuff of knowledge.

According to Ibn Sīna, the emergence of the soul or vital principle as an 'extra-corporeal power' is the result of the combination of the elements, in various degrees of 'moderation', under the influence of the heavenly bodies. First the vegetative, then the animal and finally the human soul arise in progression, depending on the degree of moderation peculiar to each. The vegetative soul is defined as the principle of growth and reproduction, the animal soul as that of motion and the apprehension of particulars, the human soul as that of deliberation and the apprehension of universals. The general definition of the soul is then given, along well-known Aristotelian lines, as 'the first perfection of an organic natural body',[14] in so far as it apprehends particulars and moves at will (as animal soul), apprehends universals and acts by deliberation or choice (as human soul) or finally is begotten, grows and reproduces its kind (as vegetative soul).

The human soul, which marks for Ibn Sīna the zenith of the biological or generative process, has two major divisions, a theoretical and a practical one. The theoretical has four subdivisions, potential or possible, habitual, actual and acquired, representing the four degrees of intellectual apprehension (*idrāk*), as distinct from sensuous apprehension, of which the soul is capable. They further represent the way in which the human intellect rises from the sheer disposition or potentiality to learn, through the acquisition of the *habitus* (*malakah*) to learn, once actualized, to the complete apprehension of universals through conjunction (*ittiṣāl*) with the Active Intellect, which, as we have seen, dominates or governs the sublunary world. When the soul has reached that stage, it will have achieved its perfection and have become, writes Ibn Sīna,

> an intelligible world in which are inscribed the form of the whole, the rational order of the whole and the good pervading the whole. It starts with the First Principle of the whole, followed by the noble substances, the pure spiritual entities, those spiritual entities connected to bodies in some way [i.e. animal and human souls] and ends with the heavenly bodies with their many forms and powers.[15]

In short, it becomes a replica of the intelligible world of which the material world is simply a reflection. This mystical stage is attained when the soul has achieved such a measure of conjunction with the Active Intellect as to dispense with the syllogistic process of reasoning altogether, and is able to apprehend universals directly through intuition (*ḥads*). Ibn Sīna describes this stage as 'prophetic' or a function of 'holy reason', marking the highest human faculty, the exclusive prerogative of philosophers and prophets. The latter are able, thanks to this faculty, to apprehend the totality of all things in an intuitive way, to perceive auditory and visual forms or representations and to foretell the future. They are even able to influence the course of events miraculously in the physical world.[16] It is noteworthy that holy reason is for Ibn Sīna a form of habitual reason, of which 'acquired reason' is the consummation.

A characteristic feature of Ibn Sīna's psychology is the hierarchical order, in which the lower powers always subserve the higher. Thus, the external senses subserve the internal, which in turn subserve the rational. First, the *sensus communis*, which co-ordinates the data received from the five external senses, subserves the imaginative power, which subserves the productive, which subserves the estimative (*al-wāhimah*), which subserves the retentive. The external senses themselves are subserved by the 'motive' powers of desire and anger designated, in line with Plato's tripartite theory of the soul, the concupiscent and the irascible, to which the 'motor', or muscular powers are subservient.[17]

The ultimate fate of the soul, as already mentioned, consists in achieving 'conjunction' with the Active Intellect, whereby it perceives the beauty and goodness of the intelligible world. Therein, Ibn Sīna was convinced, lies the true happiness of the soul. He had enough sense, however, to recognize that this sublime fate was reserved to the privileged few, or the philosophers and prophets. The souls of 'simpletons and idiots', he believed, were unable to attain that stage, either because they were unprepared by nature or by reason of sheer torpor or ineptitude. Accordingly, they would survive the destruction of the body, but would experience, due to their separation from their bodies, the utmost agony, or the inability to partake of bodily pleasures. However, the kind of happiness or misery reserved for those unfortunate souls was not, for Ibn Sīna, a matter of philosophical discourse; 'it can only be demonstrated by recourse to the Holy Law (*Sharī'ah*) or assent to prophetic report'. Ibn Sīna thus accords a certain measure of credibility to religious truth, but clearly regards it as lying outside the scope of philosophical discourse. It is presumably an inferior type of truth, accessible to the masses at large, and is received on faith in prophetic reports or instructions.

The Brethren of Purity

The interest of Muslim philosophers and historians of ideas in Neopythagoreanism may be said to have been triggered off by the profoundly religious and mystical character of that late Hellenistic movement, with which Neoplatonism tended to merge. Pythagoras (d. *c.*497 BCE) was himself one of the few pre-Socratic figures on whom the historians of ideas dwelt; he is said to have received instruction in wisdom from Solomon and in geometry from the Egyptians.[18] Moreover, the two leading Neopythagoreans, Nicomachus of Gerasa (first century CE) and Jamblichus (d. 330), who were of Syrian origin, were well known to those historians, and the former's *Introduction to Arithmetic*, translated into Arabic by Thabit Ibn Qurrah, has actually survived. Equally important in this connection is the role that Jamblichus' teacher, Porphyry of Tyre (d. 303), played, as a major interpreter of Plotinus and commentator on Aristotle's *Nicomachean Ethics*, as reported only in the Arabic sources.

When the 'Abbāsid caliphate began to disintegrate in the tenth century, secret Ismā'ili or extreme Shī'ite movements began to preach, with the support of the rival Fatimid caliphate of Egypt, a revolutionary political creed, whose philosophical and religious base was Neopythagorean and Neoplatonic. In their commitment to the general Shī'ite belief that the 'hidden' religious truth could only be unravelled by the infallible teacher or Imam, the Ismā'ilis found a welcome ally in Greek philosophy, especially in its Neopythagorean esoteric leanings, coupled with a shared obsession with mathematics as a sure pathway to truth. It is not without significance that Ibn Sīna himself tells us in his autobiography that he was first exposed to philosophy as a result of discussions of the subjects of the soul and reason according to the teachings of Ismā'ilism, to which both his father and brother had been won over, 'in reponse to the Egyptian call'.

'My father', adds Ibn Sīna, 'was in the habit of reading and reflecting upon the *Epistles of the Brethren of Purity*, and so did I at times.'[19]

These 'Epistles' (*Rasā'il Ikhwān al-Ṣafā*) embodied the philosophical, mathematical and political teachings of the Brethren of Purity, who professed an Ismā'ilism couched in a popular philosophical idiom. This secret society appeared first in Basrah in southern Iraq, then spread outwards throughout the eastern Islamic world and Muslim Spain. Its aims, as defined in the fifty-one *Epistles* which bear its name, were the quest for truth and contempt for worldly goods. Although anonymous, the names of six writers of the *Epistles* are given in the Arabic sources, of whom Abū Sulaymān al-Basti, also known as al-Maqdisi, is the most important, since he is reported to have been their actual writer or compiler. These *Epistles* form a genuine encyclopaedia of the philosophical sciences, at the centre of which lies mathematics. The motto of its authors is stated in these all-embracing words, as the refusal 'to disavow any science, discard any book or favour any one creed; since [their creed] encompasses all the creeds, sensible or rational, from beginning to end, its inner or outer parts and its overt or covert aspect ... in so far as they all derive from a single Principle, a single Cause, a single world and a single soul'.[20]

The contents of the fifty-one *Epistles*, to which a compendium was later added, written probably by al-Majrīti (d. 1008) who is said to have brought the *Epistles* into Muslim Spain, may be divided into four groups.

The first group consists of fourteen 'mathematical' epistles dealing with number, which the Brethren regarded as an essential tool for the study of philosophy, 'since the science of number', writes the author, 'is the root of all the other sciences, the essence of wisdom, the source of every cognition and the element of all meanings'.[21] The first epistle of this first group forms a prelude, the second deals with geometry, the third with astronomy, the fourth with music, the fifth with geography, the sixth with 'harmonic proportions', the seventh and eighth with the theoretical and practical arts, the ninth with ethics and the last five with the five parts of Aristotelian logic, namely the *Isagoge*, the *Categories*, the *Interpretation*, *Analytica priora* and *Analytica posteriora*. This tabulation of the sciences referred to as mathematical clearly illustrates the eclecticism of the Brethren.

The second group deals with 'physical and corporeal questions' and consists of seventeen epistles corresponding roughly to Aristotle's physical treatises, with the addition of psychological, epistemological and linguistic questions not included in the Aristotelian corpus.

The third group of ten 'psychological–rational' epistles deals with intellectual principles, the intellect as such, intelligibles, the nature of erotic love (*'ishq*), resurrection and so on.

The fourth group of fourteen epistles deals with such questions as the way to know God, the creed of the Brethren and their way of life, the nature of the divine law, the conditions of prophethood, the actions of spiritual beings, jinn and angels, political regimes and finally the nature of magic, amulets and talismans.

The mathematical teaching of the Brethren is explicitly stated to derive from Nicomachus of Gerasa and Pythagoras, 'who was a monotheistic sage who hailed from Ḥarrān'.[22] A large part of this teaching centres round their number-theory or analysis of the properties of number, starting with the number 'one'. The real 'one', according to them, is synonymous with the term 'thing' (*shay'*), which is the most general term, and is indivisible. Multiplicity arises from the addition of one to one in succession, so that 'one' may be regarded as the ground of all number, but is not itself a number. Taken as a whole, numbers are then said to possess certain physical and metaphysical properties which enable them to serve as clues to the understanding of the world and lead the diligent searcher to the knowledge of the soul, the spiritual world and ultimately God. Thus, number four, they state by way of illustration, was intended by God to reflect the quadruple reality of the spiritual world, which consists of the Creator, the universal intellect, the universal soul and prime matter. That is why He caused the elements to consist of four, the basic 'natures', or primary qualities of classical physics, the humours, the seasons, the corners of the earth and so on, all to consist of fours or quadruples.

The physical world, according to the Brethren, is an emanation from God, who created from 'the light of His unity' a simple substance, which is the Active Intellect, followed by the universal Soul of the spheres and finally prime matter. He then created the subordinate entities of the world from matter, through the agency of the Soul and the Intellect. God may, therefore, be spoken of as the First Principle of all things, in exactly the same way that the number 'one' is spoken of as the first principle of all number.

The general properties of number, according to the Brethren, are not purely conventional or conceptual; they derive from the very nature of things, or are ontological. Thus, number seven, for instance, is a perfect number, since it is the sum of the first odd number, or three, and the first square number, or four. Eight is a cubic number, since its root, which is two, multiplied by its double, which is four, makes eight. It may also be called the first solid number, because it consists of a series of planes, and the plane consists of adjacent lines. Now, the line consists of a minimum of two points, and the smallest body of two planes, so that the smallest body will consist of eight parts. For, if we multiply the line by itself, that is two by two, we would have a plane, which consists of four parts, and if we multiply the plane by one of its sides, we would have a solid, totalling eight parts, or two in length, two in breadth and two in depth.

In the light of its ontological status, the obsession of the author (or authors) of the *Epistles* with number is justified on the ground that the properties of number are paradigms of the property of all existing things. 'So that whoever understands number, its rules, its nature, its genera, its species and its properties is able to understand the multitude of the genera and species of all things, the wisdom underlying their appropriate quantities and the reason why they are neither more nor less than they are.' The answer given by the author is that God, who is the Maker of all things, being one in every sense, 'did not regard it as wise that all things should be one in every respect, or multiple in every respect ... Therefore, He arranged them in such a way that they are one with respect to matter, but multiple with respect to form.'[23] Nor did He regard it as wise that all things should be dual, triple, quadruple, etc., but rather that they should reflect the properties of number in the greatest variety of ways.

At the epistemological and religious levels, the great advantage of the study of number, according to the Brethren, is that it leads to the knowledge of the soul, in which numbers subsist, and this knowledge leads ultimately to the knowledge of God, which is possible only through philosophy. This is confirmed by the Prophetic Hadith, 'He who knows himself [in Arabic, his soul] will know his Lord.' The other advantage is that the knowledge of the soul will lead to the refinement of character and sharpening of the mind. A child born under an 'auspicious sign of the zodiac' will, upon coming of age, find that his or her soul is able to discover the truth about its essence as a spiritual substance. The soul will then strive to regain its original abode in the intelligible world 'through the profession of spiritual divine creeds', and also through 'discourse on noble philosophical matters, according to the Socratic path, while practising mysticism, asceticism and monasticism, according to the Christian path, and clinging to the Hanafi religion [i.e. Islam]'.[24]

Thereupon the soul will perceive 'those spiritual forms, glimpse those luminous substances and see those hidden matters and profound mysteries which cannot be apprehended through the bodily senses or corporeal organs. They can only be perceived by him whose soul has been purified by means of the refinement of his character.' Otherwise, the soul will not be able to 'ascend to the higher world of the spheres ... or receive those blessings which Hermes Trismegistus received through philosophy, and to which Aristotle, Pythagoras, Christ and Muḥammad bear witness'.[25]

Among the insights which an individual's self-knowledge will yield from contemplation of the multiplicity of things outside or created entities is the recognition of the intermediate position, between the infinitely large and the infinitesimally small, that humankind occupies in this vast universe, as Pascal was later to put it. Thus, the human body, compared to other objects, is neither too large nor too small; human life-span neither too long nor too short; the human position on the ladder of creation neither too high nor too low; for humans are indeed in an intermediate position between the angels and the beasts, and their knowledge is intermediate between total ignorance and total omniscience.

The conclusions that the author of the *Epistles* draws from the contemplation of humankind's position in the universe are also similar to Pascal's conclusions. The human mind, according to the *Epistles*, is unable to grasp the highest realities such as God's essence or His majesty, the form of the whole universe, or even the intelligible forms, as separated from matter. Nor are individuals able to grasp such philosophical questions as the origination of the universe and the cause of its coming into being, or the mode of existence proper to created entities in the higher or lower worlds. If the knowledge of all those realities cannot be attained through reason, the individual's only recourse is assent to the teachings of the prophets, who receive their inspiration from God, and submission to their authority, just as they have themselves submitted to the authority of the angels, their commanders and guardians.[26] Nevertheless, the author of the *Epistles* is convinced that there is no serious conflict between philosophy and religion; for their common aim is 'the imitation of God, according to human capacity'. This harks back to Plato's famous *homoiosis Theo*, quoted by al-Kindi and others as the proper definition of philosophy.[27] This imitation, according to the author, may be achieved either through theoretical knowledge or through the practice of virtue, whereby the individual attains perfection. The differences between philosophy and religion actually bear on subsidiary matters, or the peculiar idioms used by each, which are often commensurate to the understanding of the hearer. The chief merit of philosophy, according to the *Epistles*, is that it enables us to probe the hidden (*bātin*) meaning of revealed texts and teaches us not to stop at their external (*ẓāhir*) meaning in the manner of the vulgar and the profligate. It bids us understand that 'the essence of irreligion (*kufr*), error, ignorance and blindness' is to be content with external interpretations of revealed references to carnal pleasures or gross punishments. For the true sage, those references are pure allegories for spiritual truths. Thus, Hell, according to the author of the *Epistles*, is nothing other than the world of generation and corruption, lying beneath the moon, whereas Paradise is 'the abode of spirits and the vastness of the universe'. The author then cites as instances of false religious beliefs the view of the Christians that God was killed by the Jews, that of the Jews that God is an angry and jealous God and, finally, that of Muslims that God will order the angels on the Last Day to cast sinners into a ditch of fire and summon the righteous to partake of carnal pleasures, such as the deflowering of virgins, the drinking of alcohol and the eating of roast meat.[28]

The diffusion of philosophical culture in the tenth century

The *Epistles* of the Brethren of Purity clearly highlighted the need to go beyond the external or literal meaning of religious texts, including the Qur'an, and to espouse the cause of philosophy as the principal means of achieving this goal. Their occultism, on the other hand, was prompted in part by political motives and the desire to avoid public exposure, by recourse to anonymity or dissimulation (*taqiyah*) at a time when the political and religious confrontation between the western or Sunnite wing and the eastern or Shīʿite wing of the Muslim empire was at its keenest. However, what characterized the *Epistles* from a philosophical point of view was the popular style their writers adopted and the urge to avoid the use of technical terminology or grapple with abstruse or abstract concepts. Above all, they proclaimed their conviction of the unity of truth and the duty of the conscientious searcher to shun no science and disdain no book, religious or other, but to draw on all sources of scientific and religious truth, whether Persian or Indian, Jewish or Christian, Greek or other. Nevertheless, it cannot be denied that the *Epistles* are marked by a clear eclectic and rhapsodic character, which greatly detracts from their value as systematic philosophical treatises.

Of the leading authors of this period who were in close touch with the Brethren of Purity, we might mention Abū Sulaymān al-Sijistāni (d. *c.*1000), nicknamed the Logician. He was well versed in Greek philosophy and leader of an influential philosophical and literary circle. As an instance of his Greek learning, we might mention his *Suwān al-Ḥikmah* (Vessel of Wisdom), one of the earliest histories of Greek philosophy, upon which later historians of ideas have drawn, as well as numerous commentaries on Aristotelian logic which are no longer extant. His best-known disciple, Abū Ḥayyān al-Tawḥīdi

(d. 1024), was one of the leading littérateurs of the period, a man of vast philosophical culture. In some of his literary works he preserved the philosophical views of some of his predecessors and contemporaries such as Yaḥia Ibn 'Adi (d. 974), Miskawayh (d. 1030) and his own teacher, al-Sijistāni. In one of his books, *al-Imtā-'wa'l-Mu'ānasah* (Entertainment and Conviviality), he kept a record of a historic debate which took place in 932 in Baghdad between Abū Bishr Mattā, the leading logician of his day, and Abū Sa'īd al-Sirāfi, an eminent grammarian, in the presence of the vizier Ibn al-Furāt. This debate turned on the question whether the study of Aristotelian logic, a foreign importation, was really necessary for an Arab or a Muslim aiming at the mastery of 'sound speech', which is fully vouchsafed by the mastery of Arabic grammar. Echoes of this debate ring in philosophical quarters during this period and beyond, and even al-Fārābi, the greatest logician of Islam, was forced to respond to the claims of the grammarians that grammar was an adequate substitute for logic as a pre-condition of 'sound speech'. Like Abū Bishr Mattā, who was his own teacher, al-Fārābi dwells on the fundamental differences between grammar, which deals with conventional terms and constructions varying from nation to nation and from language to language, and logic, which deals with universal concepts and the universal rules for their combination.

Two other philosophers of the period should be mentioned because of the vast scope of their erudition. The first, Yaḥia Ibn 'Adi, was a skilled logician and translator of philosophical texts. In addition, he was the first philosopher to write a systematic treatise on ethics, *Tahdhīb al-Akhlāq* (Refinement of Character), and a large number of Christian theological treatises of great historical significance. Foremost of these is his rebuttal of the arguments in al-Kindi's lost 'Refutation of the Trinity' (*al-Radd 'alā al-Tathlīth*), his treatises on the *Incarnation*, the *Unity of God* and the *Refutation of the Arguments of Those who Claim that*

(Human) Acts are Created by God and Acquired by the Servants, which appears to be a refutation of the Ash'arite concept of acquisition (*kasb*).

The second, his near-contemporary, Abū 'Ali Aḥmad Miskawayh, is the greatest moral philospher of Islam, whose influence continued well into the fifteenth century, especially in Persia. In his own *Tahdhīb al-Akhlāq* and other ethical treatises he gave the most thorough analysis of Aristotelian ethical theory, grounded in Platonic psychology, with a Neoplatonic capping. In addition, we owe to Miskawayh a history book, *Tajārib al-Uman* (The Experiences of Nations); a collection of Persian, Greek, Indian and Islamic aphorisms entitled *Jāwidān Khirad* (Eternal Wisdom) and a number of psychological and ethical tracts, of which the *Orders of Happiness*, the *Essence of Justice* and *On Pleasure and Pain* are the most noteworthy.

Those philosophers illustrate the extent of the diffusion of philosophy in tenth- and eleventh-century intellectual and literary circles, as well as the ongoing controversies between the pro-philosophical and the anti-philosophical parties during this period. These controversies would continue well into the later parts of the eleventh century and beyond. During the latter period, they would acquire added virulence due to the theological and political polarization and strife they would generate. Ash'arite theology and traditionalism were pitted against philosophy, on the one hand, and dialectical or deductive methods of discourse associated with philosophy, on the other.

5

Interactions of philosophy and dogma

The eclipse of theological rationalism

Systematic theology, or *Kalām*, which we associate with the rise of the Mu'tazilite movement in the ninth century, received its chief intellectual impetus from Greek philosophy and, to a lesser extent, contact with Christian theology; and its political impetus from the patronage and zealous support of the 'Abbāsid Caliph al-Ma'mūn and his two immediate successors. Before long, however, these two circumstances proved disastrous for the cause of theological rationalism. The instinctive suspicion of the masses that philosophy, a foreign importation, was inimical to Islam, coupled with the serious but subtle reservations of such eminent scholars as al-Sijistāni and al-Tawḥīdi, who were not innocent of philosophical culture, reinforced popular belief in the hazards inherent in philosophical discourse. Philosophy and religion, according to al-Sijistāni and al-Tawḥīdi, stemmed from two different sources and were therefore impossible to reconcile. Religious belief was a matter of divine revelation and required none of the skills of philosophers, logicians or astrologers; otherwise the Qur'an would have exhorted us to cultivate those skills. Others, more competent than the Brethren of Purity, adds al-Tawḥīdi in *al-Imtā' wa'l-Mu'ānasah*, have attempted to reconcile philosophy and religion without success, and even Christians and Magians never resort to philosophy in their disputes.[1]

At the political level, the espousal of the Mu'tazilite cause by al-Ma'mūn, who, in 827 and 833, instituted the notorious Miḥnah to test the adherence of religious judges (*qadis*) to the Mu'tazilite maxim of the created Qur'an, alerted religious opinion, especially in traditionalist quarters, to the dangers of the unholy alliance of religion and politics. The standard-bearer of the opposition to al-Ma'mūn's pro-Mu'tazilite policies was the great divine and scholar Aḥmad Ibn Ḥanbal (d. 855), who stood fast against the Caliph's policies and would hear of no compromise at any cost. For Ibn Ḥanbal, the Qur'an was the uncreated and eternal Word of God and any questioning of this article of faith was tantamount to blasphemy. All attempts at reconciliation were dashed against the rock of Ibn Ḥanbal's inflexible stand. Upon the accession of al-Mutawakkil in 847, the theological policies of the state were reversed and the stage was set for the rise of the first major post-Mu'tazilite theological movement, that of Ash'arism.

Abū'l-Ḥasan al-Ash'ari (d. 935), the founder of this movement, was a Mu'tazilite up to the age of forty, when the Prophet, we are told in the classical sources, appeared to him in a dream and urged him to 'take charge' of the Muslim community (*ummah*). Thereupon, he mounted the pulpit at the Basrah Mosque and proclaimed his recantation from the 'follies and scandals' of the Mu'tazilah. However, unlike Mālik Ibn Anas (d. 795) and Aḥmad Ibn Ḥanbal, who had repudiated systematic theology (*Kalām*) altogether, al-Ash'ari continued to favour engaging in theological discourse, as the very title of his famous treatise, *Istiḥsān al Khawd fi 'Ilm al-Kalām* (The Vindication of the Use of the Science of *Kalām*), clearly implies. In this book, he approves of the use of logical deduction (*qiyās*) on the ground that the Qur'an recommended it and the Prophet himself had practised it. The many references in the Qur'an to the attributes of God, the questions of motion and rest, body and accident, with which the Prophet himself was fully familiar, were proof of this. The Qur'an and Hadith, however, according to al-Ash'ari, tended to be restrained in their use of methods of deduction, because the Muslim community had not, at that early stage, come into contact with foreign nations or religious creeds or been exposed to the problems and doubts that eventually forced the theologians to resort to them, especially in matters over which the Qur'an and Hadith were silent. It is the duty of every 'reasonable Muslim', writes al-Ash'ari, to refer in such matters 'to the body of principles, consecrated by reason, sense-experience or common sense', as well as the explicit pronouncements of the Qur'an and Hadith.[2]

On the more substantive issues that the Mu'tazilite theologians had raised, al-Ash'ari tended to tread a middle course between the traditionalists such as Mālik Ibn Anas and Aḥmad Ibn Ḥanbal, and the rationalists such as the Mu'tazilah and the philosophers. Thus, on the question of divine attributes, he rejected the views of the anthropomorphists (*mushabbihah*) and the corporealists (*mujassimah*), who, like the Shī'ite Hishām Ibn al-Hakam and 'Abdullah Ibn Karrām, had argued that the divine attributes mentioned in the Qur'an should be taken literally; or who, like Mālik, regarded questioning them a form of heresy. This famous jurist of Madinah is reported to have said, in answer to the question of whether God 'sits on the Throne', as the Qur'an puts it: 'The sitting is well known, its modality is unknown; believing it is an obligation and questioning it is a heresy (*bid'ah*)'.[3]

Although close to Mālik's view, al-Ash'ari's is more nuanced. The essential attributes of God, such as knowledge, power and life, according to him, subsist in God's essence (*dhāt*) eternally, but cannot be said to be, as the Mu'tazilah had maintained, identical with this essence or distinct from it; since the mode of predicating them of God is unknown. This thesis became known as *bilā kayfa*, or 'ask not how'. His chief objection to the Mu'tazilite view was that to argue that the attributes of God were identical with His essence would render the attributes of God equivalent to His essence, so that one could address his petitions to God's power, His knowledge or His life, instead of God Himself.[4]

On the question of free will and predestination, al-Ash'ari rejected outright the Mu'tazilite thesis that individuals, as free agents, were the creators of their deeds, on the ground that this claim was tantamount to polytheism (*ishrāk*), or at least dualism. For that reason, he charged the Mu'tazilites with being the Manichaeans or Magians (*Majus*) of Islam. According to him, God's power was absolute and His decrees irreversible.

He writes in *al-Ibānah*:

> We believe that God has created everything by bidding it simply to be, as He says [Qur'an 16, 42]: 'Indeed, when We will a thing, Our only utterance is: Be, and it comes to be'; and that there is nothing good or evil on earth except what God has willed ... [we hold] that no one can do anything before he actually does it, dispense with God or escape His knowledge; that there is no creator but God, and that man's deeds are created and pre-ordained by God, as He says [Qur'an 37, 94]: 'He created you together with what you do', and that the servants cannot create anything, but are themselves created ... that God can reform the unbelievers (*kāfirūn*) and show them mercy, so as to become believers instead; but He actually wanted them to be unbelievers, as He foreknew, has abandoned them and sealed their hearts. [We believe] that good and evil are the result of God's decree and pre-ordination (*qaḍā' wa qadar*), good or evil, sweet or bitter, and we know that what has missed us could not have hit us, or what has hit us could not have missed us, and that the servants are unable to profit or harm themselves upon it without God.[5]

Despite the stark predestinarian implications of this statement, which stands out as an eloquent proclamation of his credo, al-Ash'ari continued to struggle with the baffling question of free will and predestination, and in the process to formulate, on the basis of ambiguous Qur'anic passages, a thesis known as acquisition (*kasb*). According to this obscure thesis, intended apparently as an intermediate position between the rigid predestinarian position (*jabriyah*) of the traditionalists and the libertarian position (*qadariyah*) of the Mu'tazilah, humans are able to distinguish between necessary or compulsory actions such as trembling or convulsion and those that are voluntary. The latter are the result of humanity's created power or capacity, but in reality are the product of God's creative power. Such actions, then, may be said to be created by God, but 'acquired' by humans, for which they are deserving of punishment or reward.

This Ash'arite compromise raised as many questions as it answered. It continued to preoccupy the most subtle theologians, such as al-Bāqillāni (d. 1013), al-Baghdādi (d. 1037), al-Juwayni (d. 1086) and other Ash'arite scholars, who refined upon it in a variety of ways. They were unanimous, to begin with, that humans were unable, prior to revelation (*sam'*), solely through the light of natural reason to discriminate between right and wrong, which was the exclusive prerogative of God. Thus, right, according to those theologians, was simply that which God had explicitly commanded in the Qur'an, wrong that which He had prohibited. It followed that to predicate justice or injustice of God's actions, as the Mu'tazilah had so vehemently done, was purely presumptuous; for those two categories were nothing but arbitrary human conventions, which could not be applied to God. As the Lord of Lords, God was not subject to any superior authority, and His actions were not susceptible of any such human designations.

In an attempt to rationalize their rigid theodicy, the Ash'arites of the second generation, starting with al-Bāqillāni, developed an elaborate atomic theory, with Greek and Indian overtones. According to this theory, which was presented as the antithesis of the Aristotelian view of the physical world, everything in the world, which al-Bāqillāni simply defines as 'anything other than God', is made up of atoms and accidents. The atom (*juz'*) they then defined as the 'bearer' of accidents. They recognized a long list of positive and negative accidents, of none of which is an atom ever 'denuded', as their favourite Arabic expression has it. Those accidents might also be divided, according to them, into primary and secondary. The former consisted of the four modes or states of being (*akwān*), i.e. motion and rest, composition and position, which are inseparable from body. Al-Ash'ari himself appears to have assigned to this category of primary accidents such accidents as heat or its opposite, life or its opposite, etc. Secondary accidents differed from the former in that they were separable from body by way of transformation or change, and included such accidents as taste, smell, length, breadth and the like.

The most important property of the Ash'arite accidents is their impermanence or transiency (*fanā'*), so much so that al-Bāqillāni defines an accident as 'that whose permanence is impossible; it supervenes upon atoms and bodies, but ceases to exist in the second instant of its coming-to-be'.[6] He even finds support for this definition of atoms in Qur'an 8, 67 and 46, 24, which speak of 'the transient things (*a'rād*) of this world' and 'a passing cloud-burst' respectively.

To demonstrate the impermanence of accidents, al-Baghdādi, another leading Ash'arite, argues that the assertion of the opposite property of permanence would entail the impossibility of the destruction of accidents. For, if an accident is described as permanent *per se*, it would be impossible to destroy it without the supervention of its contrary upon it, and that would require the existence of a countervailing factor (*murajjiḥ*). For this reason, the Ash'arites in general maintained that the permanence of the atom itself depended on the continuous supervention of the accident of permanence (*baqā'*) upon it.

Since this accident of permanence, like the rest of the accidents, was incapable of permanence *per se*, it followed that God had to create the accidents, including the accident of permanence, continuously, so long as He wished the body in which these accidents inhere to endure.

The destruction of bodies, conversely, raised a cluster of problems with which the most skilful theologians grappled. Al-Bāqillāni, for instance, argued that when God wishes to destroy a certain bodily object, He withholds from it the two accidents of colour and mode (*kawn*) of which bodies can never be divested, and thereupon the body ceases to exist. Others held that the destruction of bodies followed instantly upon God's ceasing to create the accident of permanence in such bodies; while others still, like al-Qalānisi,[7] argued that the destruction of a body depended on God's creating in it the accident of impermanence (*fanā'*), whereupon it ceased to exist at once.

Later Ash'arite scholars continued the line of speculation inaugurated by the founder of the school and expanded or refined upon the arguments or propositions adumbrated by their predecessors. Strangely enough, however, despite the triumph of Ash'arism, which became identified with orthodoxy, the later Ash'arite scholars continued their assault on the Mu'tazilah, on the one hand, and the philosophers, on the other.

The voluminous output of later Ash'arite theologians constitutes a vast theological legacy. Of these theologians, the most noteworthy were al-Juwayni (d. 1086), author of *al-Shāmil* and *al-Irshād*; al-Ghazāli (d. 1111), author of *al-Iqtiṣād fi'l-I'tiqād*; al-Shahrastāni (d. 1153), author of *Nihāyat al-Iqdām*; al-Rāzi (d. 1209), author of *al-Arba'īn fī Uṣūl al-Dīn* and *al-Muḥaṣṣal* and, finally, al-Īji (d. 1355), author of *al-Mawāqif*. These impressive writings, together with the contributions of the earlier theologians, continued to be taught at such illustrious institutions as al-Azhar in Egypt and al-Zaytūna in Tunis for centuries and are still studied and commented upon throughout the Muslim world.

The Islamic assault on Neoplatonism

The struggle between philosophy and theology, or *Kalām*, may be said to have continued ever since Aristotelian logic found its way, through the Syriac medium, into learned circles in Islam. The theologians, as well as the grammarians, looked with suspicion on logic, with its abstract concepts and its convoluted methods of reasoning, and especially its foreign lineage. Arabic grammar and related linguistic disciplines such as rhetoric or prosody were deemed by the anti-philosophical party to be adequate, by themselves, for the acquisition of higher learning, including jurisprudence (*fiqh*), Hadith and Qur'anic commentary (*tafsīr*). Metaphysics, whether in its Aristotelian or Neoplatonic form, on the other hand, was deemed wholly inimical to the Islamic worldview and the teachings of the Qur'an. The theologians perceived fairly early that this metaphysics rested upon the twin notions of the efficacy of secondary causation and the continuity of nature. Operating in accordance with rational and uniform laws, this was accordingly irreconcilable with the Qur'anic concept of God's unlimited power and His inscrutable ways, and especially His prerogative to operate miraculously in the world. The very goals of philosophy, or the rational interpretation of the world, they also believed, were impudent attempts to probe the mysteries of creation and the supra-rational way in which God managed the physical world and human affairs.

Echoes of these anti-philosophical perceptions can be heard in the works of almost all the leading Ash'arite theologians from the time of al-Ash'ari onwards, but there is little doubt that the theologian who epitomizes the whole spirit of anti-philosophical dissent is Abū Ḥāmid al-Ghazāli, probably the greatest theologian of Islam and the most eloquent champion of Ash'arism. Born in Ṭūs in 1058, al-Ghazāli started his studies with a certain Radhkāni, then moved to Jurjān where he continued his studies with Abū'l-Qāsim al-Ismā'ili. His greatest teacher, however, was al-Juwayni, nicknamed Imām al-Ḥaramayn, with whom he studied logic, *Kalām* and philosophy. He studied Sufism with al-Farmadhi, a leading Sufi teacher of the time. As an accomplished scholar, al-Ghazāli was appointed head of the Nizāmiyah School in Baghdad. This had been founded by Niẓām al-Mulk, vizier of the Seljuks, to serve as a bastion of Sunni (Shāfi'i) dogma and a bulwark against the Ismā'ili propaganda mounted by the Shī'ite Fatimid caliphate of Egypt. Here al-Ghazāli taught jurisprudence and theology, with great success, from 1091 to 1095. However, the assassination of Niẓām al-Mulk by an Ismā'ili commando (*fidā'i*) in 1092 and the death of the Sultan Malik Shah shortly after forced him to give up a position which, as he says in his autobiography, *al-Munqidh min al-Ḍalāl* (Deliverer from Error), was not dedicated entirely to the service of God. It is possible, however, that he was prompted by fear for his own life because of his close association with Niẓām al-Mulk and the Shāfi'i cause. For ten years, he wandered in the guise of a Sufi throughout Syria, Palestine and Hijāz, but eventually returned to Nishapur, where he resumed his teaching. Five years later, in 1111, he died in his birthplace, Ṭūs.

Al-Ghazāli was particularly well equipped to undertake what one might call an Islamic assessment of Greek–Arabic philosophy. He says in his autobiography that he spent a total of three years studying all the philosophical sciences and meditating on them, while fully occupied teaching 300 students at the Nizāmiyah in Baghdad. This was in addition to the preparatory study he had undertaken with al-Juwayni in Nishapur. At the end of those three years, he writes, 'I was able, through divine assistance and the mere perusal of their [i.e. the philosophers'] books during those stolen hours to grasp the pith of their sciences.'[8]

The measure of his proficiency in philosophy may be gauged from al-Ghazāli's extant philosophical writings, including *Mi'yār al-'Ilm*, a very lucid summary of Aristotelian logic; the *Maqāṣid al-Falāsifah*, a summary of Neoplatonic philosophical teachings; and *Mizān al-'Amal*, an important ethical treatise, in which he constructs, upon a Platonic–Aristotelian base, an ethical synthesis whose capstone is mystical. We are told, however, in the preface of his onslaught on the philosophers, *Tahāfut al-Falāsifah* (The Incoherence of the Philosophers), that his aim in the first two books was simply to lay down the groundwork for the refutation of Aristotelianism, or rather Neoplatonism, as interpreted by al-Fārābi and Ibn Sīna, 'the two foremost and most reliable philosophizers in Islam', as he puts it.[9]

In this refutation, al-Ghazāli is judicious enough to distinguish between four parts of philosophy:

1. a part which has no 'bearing on religion' and should, therefore, not be questioned, namely logic, which is simply an 'instrument of thought';
2. a part which, like the former, has no direct bearing on religion but, due to its certainty, may lead the learner to assume that all the philosophical sciences attain the same degree of certainty. This science is mathematics;
3. a part which deals with political and ethical matters in an unobjectionable way, since the fine maxims and true principles found therein are ultimately derived from the teachings of the prophets or Sufi masters. The study of this part of the philosophical sciences, however, should be approached with caution;
4. a part, finally, which contains the bulk of the philosophers' errors, namely physics and metaphysics.

Al-Ghazāli then proceeds in the *Tahāfut* to summarize the main 'questions' on which the philosophers should be declared infidel or heretical, and which he reduces to twenty. The three most pernicious issues on which the philosophers should be anathematized (*takfīr*) are the eternity of the world; God's knowledge of universals, but not of particulars; and the denial of the resurrection of the body.

On the first point, al-Ghazāli asserts that the thesis of the eternity of the world entails logically that it is uncreated, and therefore has no Maker. Those philosophers who adhere to this view, like Aristotle, Ibn Sīna and Plotinus, are therefore Godless. In this context al-Ghazāli marshals a long array of logical and mathematical arguments intended to prove that the world was created in time (*hādith*, *muḥdath*) and will eventually cease to exist at the behest of its Creator.

On the second point, he accuses the philosophers of restricting the scope of God's knowledge to such an extent that 'the Lord of Lords and Cause of Causes has no knowledge whatsoever of what happens in the world', despite the fact that He has created it through His knowledge and will. Having stripped Him of the essential attributes, including the attribute of life, which is a precondition of knowledge and will, they have in fact reduced Him to the status of the dead.[10] The Qur'an itself, he adds, has stated in numerous passages that 'not a single atom's weight in the heavens or on earth is hidden from Him', as Sūrah 34, 3, puts it.

On the third point, concerning bodily resurrection, al-Ghazāli adopts a skilful strategy aimed at showing, as a first step, that the soul cannot be shown by the philosophers *demonstratively* to be immortal or indestructible, as they claim. If this is the case, then the only recourse open to them is to defer to the authority of revelation (*shar*ʿ) which asserts unequivocally that the soul, or spirit, is immortal and indestructible, as Qur'an 3, 169, clearly implies. This verse reads: 'Do not suppose that those who have died in the path of God are dead; they are rather alive with their Lord.' The Hadith which speaks of the 'spirits of the righteous being kept in the gullets of green birds suspended under the Throne' confirms this. Add to this, as al-Ghazāli then argues as a second step, that revelation does not stop at the immortality of the soul, but asserts the resurrection of the body as well. For revelation informs us that on the Day of Judgement the soul will be united to a body made up of the same matter as its original body, or of a different matter. When the soul has thus 'repossessed the instrument', or the material body to which it was originally united, the individual will not only revive, as bodily resurrection clearly implies, but will also regain forthwith the ability to experience those bodily pleasures and pains of which he or she was deprived at death. All this, al-Ghazāli adds, is bound to rebut the claims of the philosophers that bodily pleasures and pains, to which ample reference is made in the Qur'an, are impossible.[11]

The remaining questions of the *Tahāfut* need not detain us long. Question Seventeen, however, which bears on the necessary connection of causes and effects, deserves special mention because, as we have already mentioned, it was one of the major issues which pitted the Ash'arite theologians against the philosophers. According to al-Ghazāli, then, the alleged 'correlation between what is customarily believed to be a cause and what is believed to be an effect is not necessary, according to us'.[12] It is simply born of ingrained habit which instils in the mind the notion of necessary correlation, such as the correlation between eating and satiety, drinking and the quenching of thirst, contact with fire and burning. The only evidence in support of the allegedly necessary correlation between these and similar events in medicine and the arts is simply observation (*mushāhadah*). If we examine this matter carefully, however, we will find, according to al-Ghazāli, that observation does not prove that the alleged effect, in each such case, occurs due to the alleged cause, but only subsequently to it (*ma'ahu, lā bihi*), or that it cannot have some other cause. It is not impossible, for instance, that it could be caused by God, either directly or through the agency of the angels, 'charged with the affairs of this world', as he says.

The philosophers themselves, he adds, assert that the ultimate causes of natural occurrences in the world of generation and corruption are the separate intelligences, of which the Active Intellect, from which the substantial forms emanate, is, according to them, the supreme example.

The denial of necessary causation, it should be recalled, was proclaimed with such insistence by Ash'arite theologians, including al-Ghazāli, for one principal reason: to vindicate, as al-Ghazāli puts it in the preface to Question Seventeen of the *Tahāfut*, 'the consensus of all Muslims' that God can act miraculously in the world, and that there are no possible limits to the way in which He can operate freely in the world of which He is the Supreme Lord.

6

Philosophy and mysticism

Ascetic beginnings

Mysticism may be described as the urge to reach out to the Infinite. This may be in some mode of intellectual communion or 'conjunction', as in Neoplatonism; or through some kind of visionary illumination (*mukāshafah*, or *ishrāq*), as in the moderate forms of Islamic mysticism; or finally in a total dissolution of personal identity (*fanā'*), as in Hinduism and the 'extravagant' forms of Sufism.

The first stage in the development of Islamic mysticism, as early as the seventh century, coincides with the appearance of individual devotees or ascetics who dedicated themselves to a life of piety (*wara'*), submission (*khushū'*) or reflection (*fikr*) on the human condition and the worshipper's relation to God, described by the Qur'an as 'nearer to him than the jugular vein' (Qur'an 50, 15). Thus, during this early period there arose ascetic and unworldly circles which congregated around men of exceptional piety or learning such as al-Ḥasan al-Baṣri (d. 728). He is reported in later Sufi sources to have said, summing up this nascent religious spirit, that 'a grain of piety is better than a thousand weights of fasting and prayer', and to have defined devotion (*khushū'*) as fear constantly clinging to the heart and asceticism (*zuhd*) as contempt for the world and everything therein, whether it be people or material possessions.[1] There soon grew around al-Baṣri a circle of ascetics, both male and female. The most famous was Rābi'ah al-'Adawiyah (d. 801), who dedicated herself to the life of piety and meditation and introduced for the first time in Muslim history the concept of divine love as a pivotal point in the religious life of the devotee. Asked once whether she loved God and hated the Devil, she replied: 'My love of God has prevented me from the hatred of Satan,' or, according to another version: 'My love of God Almighty has filled my heart to such an extent that there is no room left [in it] for the love or hate of anyone else.'[2] She also expressed her love of God in these beautiful lines:

> I love You with two loves, a love of passion
> And a love prompted by Your worthiness of that.
> As for the love of passion,
> It consists in occupying myself with remembering You and no one else.
> And as for the love of which You are worthy,
> It consists in Your lifting the veils, so that I may see You.
> However, mine is not the merit in this or that,
> But Yours is the merit in this and that.[3]

However, the mystical movement's centre soon moved from Basrah to Baghdad and the next century produced some of the greatest figures in the early history of Islamic mysticism, or Sufism. Foremost among these were al-Muḥāsibi (d. 857), Ibn Abi al-Duniya (d. 894), Ma'rūf al-Karkhi (d. 815) and Abū'l-Qāsim al-Junayd (d. 911). Al-Muḥāsibi and al-Junayd deserve special mention as seminal figures in the history of Sufism. The former was born in Basrah, then moved to Baghdad where he came into conflict with the Ḥanbalites, since he was not averse to using theological arguments in his sermons. His mysticism rested on two pillars: self-examination (*muḥāsabah*) (hence his own name) and readiness to bear the worst hardships or calamities for the sake of God, the First Beloved. The true test of piety, according to al-Muḥāsibi, was the willingness to die, and that of the virtue of forbearance (*ṣabr*) was enduring excruciating pain.[4]

Abū'l-Qāsim al-Junayd, who was a disciple of al-Muḥāsibi, al-Saqaṭi (d. 870) and Abū Ḥafs al-Ḥaddād (d. 873), had the most lasting influence on subsequent mysticism in Islam. His thought is marked by a profound sense of God's transcendence and unity and the need to cling to the ritual aspect of the religious life as defined by the Holy Law, or *Sharī'ah*. For him, the basis of the spiritual life, of which mysticism is the crowning point, is the covenant (*mithāq*) into which God entered with the individual prior to his or her creation. This covenant is referred to in Qur'an 7, 171, where it is stated that 'God called upon mankind to bear witness against themselves: "Am I not your Lord?" They replied: "Yes, indeed, we bear witness."' From this covenant, it follows, according to al-Junayd, that the essence of the spiritual life is the recognition by the individual, even prior to his or her creation, while still an idea in the mind of God, of the great distance that separates humans from their Lord and Creator. Al-Junayd calls this recognition isolating (*ifrād*) the eternal from the temporal and regards it as the secret of the confession of divine unity (*tawḥīd*). This he describes as a state in which

> man becomes a ghost in the presence of the Almighty, upon whom the decrees of His providence are fulfilled in the performance of the ordinances of His power in the labyrinths of the seas of His unity, through the act of self-annihilation (*fanā'*) and oblivion of the call for creation ... so that the end of man may revert to his beginning, whereby he becomes what he was before he came to be.[5]

This notion of self-annihilation or extinction reflects clear nihilistic, Hindu influences. Before long it became the hallmark of pantheistic or 'unitary' mysticism, to which we shall now turn.

Pantheistic or unitary mysticism

The two foremost exponents of unitary mysticism, with its hyperbolic or extravagant claims, were al-Bisṭāmi and al-Ḥallāj, who pushed the idea of self-annihilation to its logical limits and contended that it logically entailed total union (*ittiḥād*). The earlier mystics, and even al-Junayd, had stopped short of this.

Abū Yazīd al-Bisṭāmi was born in Bisṭām (or Baṣām) in western Khurasān. He is said to have been schooled in mysticism at the hands of an Indian teacher, Abū 'Ali al-Sindi, who taught him, we are told, the secret of self-annihilation or extinction. A large number of his extravagant utterances (*shaṭaḥāt*) are given in the classical sources, many of them turning on the concept of intoxication (*sikr*), mystical passion (*wajd*) or union with God, implicit in which is the concept of self-deification. In one of these utterances, reported by a later Sufi, al-Bisṭāmi says:

> [God] raised me once and placed me before Him and said: 'O Abū Yazīd, My creation desires to see you.' So I said: 'Adorn me with Your I-ness and elevate me to the rank of Your uniqueness, so that when Your creation see me, they will say: "We have seen You," and then You will be that and I will not be there.'[6]

In another such utterance, he proclaims: 'Glory be to me; how great is my worth!' All the utterances attributed to him express explicitly the concept of total fusion with the divine nature, of which there are numerous instances in the Vedanta and the Upanishads.[7] Perhaps al-Bisṭāmi's most extravagant utterance is that in which he speaks of his search for God and, failing to find Him, decides to occupy His place on the Throne. In this utterance, he says:

> I plunged once into the angelic sea (*malakūt*) and the veils of divinity (*lāhūt*), until I reached the Throne, and lo, it

> was vacant. Therefore, I threw myself upon it and said: 'Lord, where will I find You?' and behold, I was I, yes, I was I. Then I returned to what I was seeking, and it was no other than I.[8]

The second outstanding figure in the history of extravagant or unitary mysticism is al-Ḥusayn Ibn Manṣūr al-Ḥallāj, who was born in al-Bayḍa', close to the shores of the Persian Gulf. He received instruction in Sufism at the hands of such eminent teachers as al-Makki (d. 909), al-Tustari (d. 986), al-Shibli (d. 945) and al-Junayd, who later dissociated himself from him, because of the extravagant streak in his character. From that point on, it appears that al-Ḥallaj embarked on a career of public speaking and active politicking, including association with the Qarmatian or Shī'ite cause. After a third pilgrimage to Makkah, he returned to Baghdad completely changed, as his son Aḥmad reported. He had reached a point in his mystical development which he described as the 'essence of union' (*'ayn al-jam'*), in which, as he claimed, the I and the Thou, the mystic and the divine object of his search, become one. His reputation spread far and wide and in 909 the vizier, Ibn al-Furāt, initiated legal proceedings against him on the ground that he was a Qarmatian agent. He was thrown in gaol shortly afterwards, remaining there for nine years. Eventually, a canonical jury convicted him on the charges of blasphemy and self-deification and the sentence was signed by the Caliph. Invoking the Qur'anic sanction that 'those who fight against God and His Apostle and work corruption in the land shall be executed, crucified, their hands and feet cut off on both sides, or driven out of the land' (Qur'an 5, 32), the vizier, Ḥāmid, in an excess of zeal, ordered him to be whipped, mutilated, crucified, decapitated, incinerated and his ashes scattered over the Tigris river. The Caliph had, in fact, merely ordered scourging and decapitation.[9]

Interactions of mysticism and Neoplatonism

The martyrdom of al-Ḥallāj was a stark reminder of the dangers inherent in the doctrine of the 'essence of union', which al-Ḥallāj interpreted as simply the manner in which the mystic becomes an instrument of God, speaking and writing on His behalf. The jury who convicted al-Ḥallāj on the charge of blasphemy (*kufr*) would not hear of such subtleties and interpreted the 'essence of union' as flagrant self-deification, which could not be tolerated.

Later mystics such as al-Ghazāli and Ibn 'Arabi took stock, perhaps, of the lesson al-Ḥallāj's execution dramatically taught. Their interpretation of the mystical experience, however extravagant or even soul-wrenching, stopped short of the claim of union with God (*ittiḥād*); instead this concept was replaced by that of the confessing of unity (*tawḥīd*) by al-Ghazāli, and by that of the unity of being (*waḥdat al-wujūd*) by Ibn 'Arabi.

Al-Ghazāli, whom we have already met as the arch-critic of Muslim Neoplatonism, tells us in his autobiography, *al-Munqidh*, that from his youth he thirsted after truth. The study of philosophy, *Kalām* and Ismā'ili esoteric (*bāṭini*) doctrine did not quench his thirst, and after years of study, teaching and reflection, he came to the conclusion that 'the Sufi adepts are primarily those who tread the path of God, their conduct being the best conduct, their route the straightest route and their character the best character.' For 'all their movements,' he adds, 'their standings still outwardly or inwardly, derive ultimately from the niche of prophetic light, and beyond prophethood, there is no light on the face of the earth, which could enlighten one.'[10]

According to al-Ghazāli the Sufi path, however, does not justify flouting the ordinances of the Holy Law, neglecting religious obligations or observances or identifying the Creator with the creature, as extravagant mystics had tended to do. The essence of mysticism, for him, as it had been for al-Junayd, his spiritual master, is simply the confession of God's unity (*tawḥīd*) or, as he sometimes puts it, 'extinction in unity'. This confession of unity really meant, for al-Ghazāli, the recognition that God was the Sole Being, the Sole Agent and the Sole Light in the universe. This Being could not be known through rational discourse or speculation, as the philosophers had claimed, or through union with Him, as al-Bisṭāmi and al-Ḥallāj had claimed. Rather, He could be known through His self-unveiling (*kashf*) in the wake of an arduous and personal process of constant observation (*mushāhadah*); that is, through the effulgence of the divine light. In one of his best-known mystical treatises, *Mishkāt al-Anwār* (The Niche of Lights), al-Ghazāli, commenting on Qur'an 24, 34, which speaks of God as 'the Light of the heavens and the earth', describes God as the Light of Lights from which all existing entities, starting with the angels and ending with terrestrial objects, derive their light and their being. However, according to al-Ghazāli, all those entities are said to exist metaphorically or figuratively; for compared to the True Being, they appear as mere non-entities, with no reality of their own. He writes:

> At this point, the mystic seers are able to rise from the plane of metaphor to that of reality, and to continue their ascent until they are able to see visually that there is no being in the world save God Almighty; and that everything is perishable except His Face, not in the sense that it becomes perishable at a given point in time, but rather that it is perishable eternally and everlastingly and could not be imagined otherwise. For everything, considered in itself, is pure nothing; but considered from the standpoint of the being which it receives from the First Reality, it appears as existing, not in itself, but rather in relation to the Face of its Maker. Thus, the only real existent is God and His

> Face; for everything has two faces, one unto itself, and one unto its Lord. With respect to itself, it is nothing, but with respect to the Face of God Almighty, it is an existing entity. Therefore, there is no existing entity, except God Almighty and His Face, and accordingly, everything is perishable save His Face, eternally and everlastingly.[11]

However, for al-Ghazāli humans occupy a pre-eminent position upon the ladder of creation; for God created them in His image and likeness and made them the epitome of the whole universe. That is why it has been said (in a Prophetic Tradition) that 'only he who knows himself knows his Lord'. The analysis of human cognitive powers, called by al-Ghazāli spiritual, shows that they begin with sense-experience and the imagination, then culminate in reason, with its two subdivisions, the intuitive and the deductive, called by him reflective. Above these powers, corresponding roughly to the philosophers' teaching, the prophets, says al-Ghazāli, attribute to humans a higher power, the 'prophetic spirit', which enables them to partake of the knowledge of the 'unseen' (*al-ghayb*), the canons of the Hereafter and other 'divine cognitions', which he does not specify.[12] It follows that the highest human cognitions are God-given, called by al-Ghazāli in *al-Munqidh* 'a light which God Almighty casts in the heart, and this light is the key to all modes of cognition'.[13] It is a form of revelation or inspiration which does not depend on carefully constructed arguments or proofs, but rather on 'God's vast mercy'.

In all the stages of knowledge mentioned above, the seers or knowers, according to al-Ghazāli, perceive God through 'a veil of light', which conceals His reality as absolute Lord or Creator who transcends all modes of qualification or relation. The highest class of knowers, called by him 'those who have arrived' (*waṣilūn*), are alone able to understand that the world of the spheres (or the celestial world of Neoplatonic cosmology), as well as their movers (or the separate intelligences), are all subject to the Creator of the heavens and the earth. He is not perceived by them, as by inferior knowers, in His capacity as 'the Obeyed One' (*muṭāʿ*), but rather as 'a Being completely divested of all that the sight of those inferiors has perceived ...; namely, as entirely hallowed and transcending everything already described'.[14]

This epistemological or cognitive theory, couched in the metaphorical language of light, of which mystics have always been very fond, culminates in a condition called by al-Ghazāli 'extinction in unity' or 'extinction in extinction'. In that condition, the mystic is so totally absorbed by the object of his contemplation that he is no longer aware of himself or of his condition. To describe this condition in *al-Munqidh*, al-Ghazāli is content to quote these romantic lines of the ʿAbbāsid poet Ibn al-Muʿtazz:

> Then there was what there was, of which I have no recollection;
> Think well [of me], then, and ask not what happened.[15]

A careful analysis of the texts, especially the *Niche of Lights*, shows that al-Ghazāli's epistemology rests upon a Neoplatonic cosmology presided over by the Obeyed One, as the mover of the heavens, who is nonetheless subordinate to the Supreme Being, 'Who has created the heavens, created the outermost sphere and created him who orders it to move'.[16] In short, this is a Being who transcends everything perceived by all those who have not attained the rank of 'those who have arrived'. Like the One of Plotinus, this Being is clearly above thought, but not above being, since all existing entities, as we have seen, derive their own being from Him. In that respect, he is closer to Ibn Sīna's Necessary Being than to Plotinus'; but in either case, al-Ghazāli, despite his assault on Neoplatonism, could not free himself from its influence. In his ethics, too, contained in *Mizān al-'Amal*, as already mentioned on p. 87, the Platonic and Neoplatonic influence is perfectly discernible.[17]

Be this as it may, the most eloquent expression of mystical experience and the mystical view of reality in Islam was probably that of Muḥyi al-Dīn Ibn 'Arabi, who was born in Murcia, Spain in 1165 and travelled extensively throughout the East before settling down in Damascus, where he died in 1240. His spiritual masters included al-Tirmidhi (d. 898), al-Wāsiṭi (d. 942) and Ibn al-'Ārif (d. 1141), as well as the philosopher-mystic Ibn Masarrah (d. 931). In 1201, we are told, 'he was ordered' to travel east, and so he set out on a journey which took him to Makkah, where he wrote his best-known work, *al-Futūḥāt al-Makkiyah* (Makkan Revelations). The list of his writings has been estimated at 846, of which some 550 have survived in printed or manuscript form.

The pivotal point of Ibn 'Arabi's mysticism, as already mentioned, is 'the unity of being', or *waḥdat al-wujūd*; but his philosophical starting-point is that of the Logos (*kalimah*) or Word. According to him, every prophet, as a symbol of the highest religious or spiritual truth, has a proper essence or reality, which Ibn 'Arabi calls his Word or Logos, and which is an expression or manifestation of the Divine Reality. But for the successive revelations of this Reality in those Words or prophetic epiphanies, he argues, the Divine Reality would have forever remained hidden. Ibn 'Arabi, then, distinguishes between the hidden aspect of the Divine Reality, which can never be grasped, and which he calls the aspect of 'uniqueness' (*aḥadiyah*) and that of 'Lordship' (*Rubūbiyah*), through which God reveals Himself to the world and becomes thereby the Lord, or Object of Worship (*Ma'būd*). The first aspect is entirely free from multiplicity or determinateness and in that respect God may be called the Pure Light, the Pure Good, or simply the Blindness (*al-'Amā*). The second aspect, however, reveals a certain measure of multiplicity or differentiation, because in it

God is both the Creator and the created, i.e. the totality of all things.[18] Multiplicity attaches to God, as he explains, by reason of His many attributes and determinations; so that, considered in Himself, He is the Reality (*al-Ḥaqq*), but considered with respect to His attributes, as revealed in contingent and created entities, He is the creation (*al-khalq*). These two aspects or manifestations of the divine essence, unity and multiplicity, necessity and contingency, Creator and created, are really one and the same.

Ibn ʻArabi then proceeds to describe creation in essentially emanationist or Neoplatonic terms. Creation existed originally in the divine mind as a series of exemplars, which he calls 'fixed entities' (*aʻyān thābitah*). God, who was hidden hitherto, now decides to reveal Himself, and so He produces the whole creation by dint of His own command (*amr*), as repeatedly mentioned in the Qur'an. This creation is related to Him as the picture to the mirror, the shadow to the person of whom it is the shadow and the number to the unit. The motive for God's decision to bring the world out of nothing, however, is not the 'necessity of nature' to which al-Fārābi and other Neoplatonists had referred, but rather love, as the Prophetic Tradition has it: 'I was a hidden treasure, then I wanted [in Arabic, loved] to be known.'[19] The primordial creation or highest manifestation of the divine nature, according to Ibn ʻArabi, is the human reality, associated with Adam, and which he calls the Adamic Logos, identified with the Perfect Man (*al-insān al-kāmil*). For him, the existence of the Adamic Logos is the *raison d'être* of the whole creation, and the Perfect Man is the visible manifestation of the Divinity. Having been created in God's image, the Perfect Man is the paragon of creation and a replica of the whole universe, which embodies all the perfections of the universe, as well as those of the divine Being Himself. This is the significance, according to Ibn ʻArabi, of humankind's designation in the Qur'an as the viceregent (*khalīfah*) of God in the world.

In this latter respect, humankind may be distinguished from all other created entities, including the angels, in so far as humans are the only beings in whom the divine attributes are fully reflected and who are capable of knowing God in a complete manner. The angels, as pure spiritual entities, are able to know Him only as a spiritual Being, whereas humans are able to know Him both as a spiritual Being, which is the Reality, on the one hand, and as the visible manifestation of this Reality, which is the creation, on the other.

In his account of the human soul, Ibn 'Arabi distinguishes, in the manner of the Neoplatonists generally, between the human or rational soul and the animal or irrational one. He rejects, however, the Neoplatonic concept of contact or conjunction (*ittiṣāl*) of the rational soul with the Active Intellect lying on the periphery of the terrestrial world. Instead, he argues that the soul, upon its separation from the body, will repair to a sphere analogous to this lower world, created by God to serve as its permanent abode. He is categorical, however, that the soul is a separate substance, entirely distinct from the body and is, in fact, a part of the spiritual world, or the 'world of Command', as the Qur'an calls it. The highest stage attainable to the human soul is the direct experiential stage (*dhawq*), which al-Ghazāli and many other Islamic mystics have regarded as the ultimate goal of the soul. This is in contrast to al-Bisṭāmi and al-Ḥallāj, who believed that this ultimate goal was union (*ittiḥād*) with God. When the soul has attained the experiential stage it will have achieved the condition of self-annihilation (*fanā'*) and will be able to perceive visually and experientially the unity of all things, the Creator and His creation, the visible and the invisible, the eternal and the temporal. Ibn 'Arabi's metaphysical pantheism was thus complete. It differed, however, from the 'unitary' mysticism of al-Bisṭāmi and al-Ḥallāj in the respect that the latter two mystics' outlook was entirely personal or existential. The unity they were both talking of was simply the unity, or rather identity, of the mystic and God, often referred to in the literature as the Beloved, or simply the Truth (*al-Ḥaqq*).

Following the death of Ibn ʻArabi, Sufism took the more practical or collective form of fraternities, in which the novices (singular, *murīd*) congregated around a master (*shaykh*). Together they engaged in the practice of prayer, meditation and repetition of the divine name (*dhikr*) in search of mystical trance. Some Sufi fraternities, known as the dancing dervishes, sought to achieve this trance through the practice of circular dancing or simply whirling around, and flourished mostly in Turkey. The earliest Sufi fraternity was founded by ʻAbd al-Qādir al-Jīli, or al-Jīlani (d. 1166). This was followed by the Rifāʻi fraternity, founded by Aḥmad al-Rifāʻi (d. 1175) and that of the Mawlawi fraternity, or dancing dervishes mentioned above. Its founder was the great Persian poet, Mawlāna Jalāl al-Dīn al-Rūmi (d. 1273), who died in Konya, Turkey, where this fraternity has continued to flourish up to the present time. Other fraternities include the order of al-Shādhili, founded by ʻAli al-Shādhili (d. 1258) and the Badawi order, founded by Aḥmad al-Badawi (d. 1276). These two orders flourished in Egypt and North Africa and continue today to have a profound religious influence in popular quarters.

In South East Asia and North Africa, Sufi orders flourished and had a profound impact on the ordinary people, who had no use for the elaborate discursive methods of the philosophers and the theologians (*mutakallimūn*) and found in mysticism, with its emphasis on the experiential path, a more adequate means of achieving religious piety in a communal milieu. This efflorescence of Sufism in the practical level is matched by the abundance of Sufi works in Malay by such eminent scholars as Ḥamzah Fansūri (d. 1600) and others, who will be discussed in chapter 10.

In North Africa, Sufism gained ground during the reign of the Almohades dynasty (1147–1269), which gave the Sufi orders official recognition for the first time in Muslim history, and authorized the study of *Kalām*, which had been banned by their predecessors, the Almoravids. A characteristic feature of North African Sufism was its Maraboutisme, or cult of saints, which spread south as far as the Niger, and east as far as Egypt. The al-Shadhiliyah order, founded by the disciples of Ali Shadhili in Tunisia, spread throughout North Africa. Some of its offshoots, such as al-Tijaniyah and al-Rahmaniyah, continue to be influential in Morocco and Algeria.

Despite the excesses to which some of the Sufi orders were prone, Sufism has continued to assert its vitality in popular quarters. A remarkable instance is the order founded by Ben 'Aliwa (d. 1934), which exerted a lot of influence on large sections of modern opinion, including European intellectuals, especially in France and Switzerland. Ben 'Aliwa's monism is very radical and outstrips even the monism of Ibn 'Arabi.

In spite of its continuing vitality, Sufism has had to contend in modern times with the most diverse rival forces, such as modernism and secularism, on the one hand, and Wahhabism and fundamentalism on the other. Each movement, for its own special reasons, has disavowed its allegiance to Sufism, either because of its stress on the inward or personal aspect of worship, or its practice of the cult of saints, mentioned above, which, interpreted as a form of intercession (*shafā'ah*), had been rejected as early as the eighth century by the Mu'tazilites themselves.

In general, the young generations of Muslims, especially those who have been exposed to Western education and ways of thinking, tend to be averse to mysticism as somewhat outmoded. Muslim intellectuals go further and reject Sufism as a form of escapism or retreat into the inner fort of the soul, as the case of Muḥammad 'Abduh (d. 1905) himself illustrates at the turn of the last century. During the twentieth century, Muslim intellectuals tended to align themselves, instead, with active European ideologies, such as Marxism, socialism, and nationalism.

7

The resurgence of Peripatetic philosophy in al-Andalus

The beginnings of philosophical speculation in al-Andalus

Partly as a consequence of the reverses it received in the Muslim East at the hands of the Ash'arites, the Ḥanbalites and others, philosophy sought a refuge in the western parts of the Muslim empire. From the eighth century the Umayyads had succeeded in founding a dynasty in Spain which, before long, was able to rival the 'Abbāsids not only politically but culturally. However, it is noteworthy that despite the political rivalries between the 'Abbāsids of Baghdad and the Umayyads of Cordova, the capital of al-Andalus (Muslim Spain), cultural contacts between East and West had continued, as the travels of Andalusian scholars eastwards clearly show.

According to the native historian of philosophy and medicine, Ṣā'id al-Andalusī (d. 1070), the study of medicine and the 'ancient sciences' in al-Andalus had started as early as the reign of the Umayyad Caliph Muḥammad Ibn 'Abd al-Raḥmān (852–66), but received fresh impetus during the reign of al-Ḥakam II, known as al-Mustanṣir (961–76). He ordered the importation of scientific and philosophical books from the East, so that during his reign Cordova began to rival Baghdad, with its university and library. Matters took an adverse turn during the reign of his successor, Hishām II (976–1009). He ordered the burning of the books on the subjects of the 'ancient sciences' that his predecessor had painfully collected, especially those on astronomy and logic, which had always been regarded as religiously suspect. However, interest in philosophy and science revived by the middle of the next century, and a number of eminent scholars distinguished themselves in these fields. Noteworthy among those scholars are 'Abd al-Raḥmān, nicknamed the Euclidean, who wrote on geometry and logic, and Abū 'Uthmān Ibn Fatḥūn, whose interests centred on music and grammar, but who is reported to have written a philosophical treatise entitled the *Tree of Wisdom*.[1]

However, the outstanding scholar of this period was Maslamah Ibn Aḥmad al-Majrīṭi (d. 1008), who travelled extensively in the East and was apparently in touch with the Brethren of Purity, whose *Epistles* he or his disciple al-Kirmāni is said to have brought to al-Andalus. According to some reports, this al-Majrīṭi is the author of the 'compendium' of these fifty-one epistles that is often appended to the collection. He is also credited with writing a treatise on physics and magic entitled *Ghāyat al-Hakīm* (The Aim of the Sage), a jumble of Hermetic, Neoplatonic and esoteric ideas, although his authorship of this work is doubtful. An earlier scholar who travelled eastwards and appears to have been drawn to Mu'tazilite theology is Ibn Masarrah (d. 931), referred to by Ṣā'id as the Esoteric (al-Bāṭini), which may be an allusion to his Ismā'ili sympathies. Upon his return from the East, he is said to have led a life of solitude and asceticism and his ideas, as already mentioned, are said to have influenced the great Andalusian mystic Ibn 'Arabi. The Spanish orientalist Miguel Asin Palacios has attributed to him and his followers a series of pseudo-Empedoclean ideas, although his thought appears to be a jumble of Neoplatonic and mystical ideas of the conventional type.

Other Andalusian scholars might be mentioned, such as

Abū'l-Ḥakam al-Kirmāni (d. 1066), disciple of al-Majrīṭi, who distinguished himself in geometry, although he is said to have also written on philosophical and logical subjects. According to one tradition, it was he, rather than his teacher al-Majrīṭi, who brought back the *Epistles of the Brethren of Purity* to al-Andalus from his Eastern travels. Ṣā'id finally singles out as scholars who were interested in philosophical and metaphysical subjects 'Abdullah Ibn al-Nabbāsh al-Bajjā'i and Abū 'Uthman of Toledo.[2]

Ibn Bājjah

Despite the scantiness of information on the subject of philosophical and scientific activity in al-Andalus, it is clear that the eleventh century witnessed the rise of a group of scholars who laid the groundwork for a genuine philosophical–scientific revolution. This would culminate in the revival of Aristotelianism and serve as a dramatic prelude to the westward transmission of Greek–Arabic philosophy. Philosophy, especially Aristotelianism, had been almost completely forgotten in Western Europe since the time of Boethius (d. 525). He had translated most of Aristotle's logical works into Latin, but it was not until the translation of Ibn Rushd's great commentaries on the whole Aristotelian corpus during the early decades of the thirteenth century that philosophy began to revive in Western Europe.

The story of Andalusian philosophy, however, starts with Abū Bakr Ibn al-Sāyigh, better known in the Arabic sources as Ibn Bājjah and in the Latin sources as Avempace. He was born in Saragossa towards the end of the eleventh century, moved to Seville and then to Granada and died of poison at a relatively young age in Fez, Morocco, in 1138. Little else is known about his life, although a disciple of his, Ibn al-Imām, transcribed a large number of his philosophical writings, and wrote a short account of his life, in which he describes Ibn Bājjah's philosophical output as 'miraculous', since 'prior to him', Ibn al-Imām says in verse, 'eyes had never seen a sun rising from the West', meaning al-Andalus.[3] This philosophical output includes a *Paraphrase of Aristotle's Physics*, a large number of glosses on al-Fārābi's logic, a political treatise entitled *The Conduct of the Solitary* and an *Epistle on Conjunction.* Although brief and often unfinished, these writings reveal a profound philosophical acumen which earned him the highest praise in certain quarters and some denigration in others.

From the start, Ibn Bājjah places himself in the mainstream of the Neoplatonic–Peripatetic tradition inaugurated in Islam by al-Fārābi, whom he appears to have chosen as his sole Eastern master in logic, politics and metaphysics. Of the other philosophers and theologians of the East, he only mentions al-Ghazāli by name, but omits any mention of Ibn Sīna or his successors. He appears to have a great affinity with al-Fārābi by reason of his ethical–political interests, which Ibn Sīna, as we have seen, had no time for. Thus, in his best-known work, *Tadbīr al-Mutawaḥḥid* (Conduct of the Solitary), his problem, like that of al-Fārābi, is to determine the type of political regime which is compatible with the philosophical life. Such a regime he argues, like Plato in the *Republic,* is one which provides the framework for a life of wisdom and virtue, worthy of the philosophers, but in no need of physicians or judges. When such an ideal state, in which disease or crime does not exist, degenerates into one of the four corrupt regimes that Plato and al-Fārābi enumerated, the plight of the philosopher therein becomes truly sorry. He will face two choices: either to emigrate to a virtuous or ideal city, if such exists anywhere, or to 'manage' his affairs as best he can, living like a stranger or 'solitary' in the midst of his own people and associates.

The management or conduct (*tadbīr*) of these affairs, which gave his famous *Tadbīr al-Mutawaḥḥid* (Conduct of the Solitary) its title, leads Ibn Bājjah to enquire into the types of action the 'solitary', or true, philosopher should seek. He is especially concerned with those likely to lead to the final condition of conjunction with the Active Intellect, which the Muslim Neoplatonists almost without exception identified with humans' ultimate felicity in this world. Human actions, according to Ibn Bājjah, may be divided into voluntary and involuntary; the latter, arising from impulse, are common to humans and beasts; whereas the former, arising from deliberation and choice, are exclusively human. In corrupt states, all actions are involuntary or impulsive because their inhabitants do not act in accordance with the dictates of reason, but rather from the desire for the necessities of life, as in al-Fārābi's necessary city; from the desire for pleasure, as in the ignominious city; or for conquest, as in tyranny.[4]

If the essence of humankind is reason, or action in accordance with the dictates of reason, rather than impulse, it follows that humans belong to the class of 'spiritual' entities or forms of which the Neoplatonists and mystics spoke. However, for Ibn Bājjah, the spiritual entities are of four types:

1. the forms of the heavenly bodies, which are entirely immaterial and by which Ibn Bājjah appears to mean the separate intelligences, which in Aristotelian and Islamic cosmology are the movers of these bodies;
2. the acquired and Active Intellects, which are equally immaterial;
3. the material forms abstracted from matter;
4. those forms or representations stored in the three internal faculties of the soul; namely, the *sensus communis*, imagination and memory, which, like the material forms, are raised to the spiritual level through the abstractive function of the soul, whose highest instance is rational thought.[5]

Almost like the Sufis, whose methods he sometimes repudiates as gross since they rest upon sensuous images or representations, Ibn Bājjah assigns humankind to the higher, spiritual realm, but only to the extent that humans are able to unite with spiritual forms, especially with the Active Intellect which is the nearest to them, so to speak. However, this union, or rather conjunction, is, for Ibn Bājjah, purely intellectual, not affective or sensuous as it was for the Sufis, who used the language of love, contemplation or vision (*mushāhadah*), as we saw in chapter 6. Moreover, its object is not the Supreme Being or God, but those subordinate spiritual entities, including the Active Intellect, that, according to the Muslim Neoplatonists, occupied an intermediate position halfway between God and the material world.

When individuals achieve the supreme condition of conjunction with the 'spiritual' or intellectual entities of the spiritual or intellectual world, their happiness will be complete. If philosophers are not able to achieve this condition because of the pressures of life in corrupt states or regimes, their lot is truly sorry and their duty as philosophers is to pursue the life of solitude, as best they can. Such a life of solitude or withdrawal from the world, Ibn Bājjah is careful to observe, does not necessarily contradict the Aristotelian maxim that humans are political animals by nature. For the life of solitude, although evil *per se*, may, under certain conditions, prove to be desirable by accident. It may be a necessary evil if humans are to attain the intellectual or spiritual ideal for which they are destined. In that respect it may be compared to bitter medicine which, although undesirable in itself, is nevertheless desirable *per accidens*.

It should be noted in this connection that the ideal of solitude Ibn Bājjah preaches in the *Conduct of the Solitary* is obviously close to the ideal of withdrawal from the world that the Sufis preached. However, he emerges in that book as a major critic of Sufism, on the ground, as we have already mentioned, that it resorts to sensuous representations in its account of the mystical experience. However, in the *Treatise on Conjunction*, he admits that above the rank of theoretical knowledge, there is a rank of the 'blessed', as he calls them, whose condition is 'too sublime to be referred to the natural process ... but deserves to be called divine, since God confers it on whomever of His servants He pleases'.[6] This apparent concession to Sufism is contradicted, however, in his *Farewell Message*, in which Ibn Bājjah reaffirms the traditional Neoplatonic view, according to which human cognitive nature reaches its consummation in the acquired intellect, as fulfilled by contact with the Active Intellect. The function of revelation itself is confined in that work to 'the fulfillment of God's noblest gift to man, i.e. rational knowledge (*'ilm*)'. For 'reason is God's dearest creation to Him ... and to the extent [the individual] is close to reason, he is close to God ... This is possible only through rational knowledge, which brings man close to God, just as ignorance cuts him off from Him.'[7]

Ibn Rushd, Ibn Bājjah's great Andalusian successor, referred in his own *Treatise on Conjunction* to Ibn Bājjah's dilemma and stated explicitly that, in subscribing to a similar view himself, he had in fact been 'induced into error' by his predecessor.[8]

Ibn Ṭufayl

The second major figure in the history of Andalusian philosophy was Abū Bakr Ibn Ṭufayl, who was born in Wādi Ash, not far from Granada, and received instruction in the medical and philosophical sciences in Seville and Cordova. He came into contact with the Almohad Caliph Abū Ya'qūb Yūsuf, who was fond of philosophy and science, and served him as his physician and counsellor. When the Caliph died in 1184, Ibn Ṭufayl continued in the service of his successor, Abū Yūsuf Ya'qūb, until his death at an advanced age in 1185.

Apart from a lost treatise *On the Soul*, the only work of Ibn Ṭufayl to have reached us is a philosophical allegory entitled *Ḥayy Ibn Yaqẓān* (Living Son of Wakeful), which was also the title of one of Ibn Sīna's mystical writings embodying his so-called 'Oriental Wisdom'. This 'Oriental Wisdom' is itself the pivotal point of Ibn Ṭufayl's own philosophy and is to be identified, according to him, with Sufism, despite the protestations of most Muslim philosophers, including Ibn Bājjah, to the contrary. Rational discourse, those philosophers held, was incompatible with the mystical experience, which its own adepts described as extra-rational and ineffable.

In *Ḥayy Ibn Yaqẓān*, then, Ibn Ṭufayl attempts to prove the thesis of the unity of rational and mystical wisdom by the use of a fictional narrative. The central figure in this narrative is Ḥayy, who was born on a desert island in the Indian Ocean, by spontaneous generation, according to one account, or from an illicit union of a princess and her lover on a neighbouring island, according to another. There, left to his own resources, the infant is given suck by a gazelle which has lost its fawn, until he grows strong enough to vie with wild beasts on the island. Eventually the gazelle dies, causing Ḥayy great distress. A crude autopsy leads him to the discovery that the death was the result of a disorder of the heart, leading to the loss of spirit, or the vital principle, without any visible corporal damage. Ḥayy concludes from these observations that death is simply the outcome of the dissolution of the union of soul and body.

Next, Ḥayy discovers, Prometheus-like, the secret of fire, which he is soon able to relate to the phenomenon of life. By degrees, his empirical observations of the composition of bodies, their corruptibility and the hierarchy of plants and animals lead him to the discovery of the spiritual world. By the age of twenty-eight, Ḥayy is able to rise to the discovery of the incorruptible world of the stars and the necessity of a Creator thereof. But whether the world was created in time, as the theologians hold, or is eternal, as the philosophers believe, he cannot decide, although he is convinced that, on either supposition, the world must have a Creator.[9] Thereupon, he proceeds to meditate on the beauty and order of the creation. He concludes that its Author must be perfect, all-knowing, all-bounteous and good; must in fact possess all the attributes of perfection of which we find instances or traces in the lower world; and, contrariwise, must be free from all imperfection.

When Ḥayy starts, at the age of thirty-five, to enquire how he has arrived at the knowledge of the Necessary Being who is entirely immaterial, he is led to conclude that it is not through any of the bodily senses, but rather through the soul that he is able to apprehend that Being, and that his soul constitutes his own essence. At this point, he becomes convinced of the nobility of the soul, its independence from the conditions of generation and corruption and the fact that its true felicity consists in total absorption in the contemplation of the Necessary Being.

Through a process of inward self-examination, Ḥayy is, then, able to discover his threefold nature: (1) by reason of his animal impulses and propensities, he is akin to the animal kingdom; (2) by reason of his spirituality, he is akin to the heavenly bodies; and (3) by reason of the nobility of his soul and its incorporeal nature, he is akin to the Necessary Being. Therefore, three duties are incumbent on him:

1. because of his kinship to the animal kingdom, he should attend to his bodily needs, but only to the extent this would enable him to fulfil his ultimate goal of contemplating God;
2. because of his spiritual or intellectual nature, he should dwell on the contemplation of the beauty and order of the universe;
3. because of his kinship to God, he should understand that the intellectual contemplation of God is not enough, because in this contemplation the soul is not able to overcome the consciousness of its own identity or selfhood.

Anyone who wishes to achieve the condition of perfect contemplation should overcome this selfhood and strive to achieve that ecstatic condition which the Sufis, like al-Ghazāli, called extinction in unity (*fanā'*), or the recognition that in reality nothing exists except the True One, and that everything, whether corporeal or spiritual, considered in itself, is really nothing. Al-Ghazāli had also contended this in the *Mishkāt al-Anwār*, as mentioned on p. 97. However, Ḥayy was guarded by divine grace against the temptation to which some Sufis, like al-Bisṭāmi and al-Ḥallāj succumbed, of imagining that in their ecstatic condition they had become identified with God or the True Reality.

In the second part of his philosophical allegory, Ibn Ṭufayl deals with the other major problem of Islamic philosophy, which had exercised the philosophers and theologians from the time of al-Kindi: the relation of reason and revelation, or philosophy and religion. According to the allegory, on a neighbouring island there lived two young men, Absāl and Salamān, who both adhered to a current religious creed, which Ibn Ṭufayl does not name. Of the two, Absāl was more intent on probing the hidden or 'inward' meaning of religious truth, whereas Salamān was more inclined to cling to the 'external' aspect of that truth. One day, Absāl lands on Ḥayy's island, teaches him language and starts to converse with him. As Ḥayy relates his own spiritual discoveries to Absāl, the latter is thoroughly impressed and begins to understand that the references in revealed scriptures to angels, prophets, Heaven and Hell are mere representations, in sensuous terms, of spiritual truths which Ḥayy has discovered on his own. Ḥayy, for his part, also discovers that everything Absāl relates to him about revelation, ritual observances, punishments and rewards fully concurs with what he himself has experienced on his own. Hence, he cannot but assent to what the Law laid down by the Prophet has taught humankind, and accept it as the unquestionable truth.

In this manner, Ibn Ṭufayl claims to be able to solve the problem of the apparent conflict between philosophy and religion, reason and faith, recognizing, like Ḥayy, that truth has two facets, so to speak, an internal and an external. Once properly understood, though, the two facets are really the same. Those two facets, in addition, correspond to the two divisions of mankind: the privileged few who are able on their own to attain the highest cognitive levels, either through philosophical discourse or mystical enlightenment (*kashf*), and the masses at large, who are not. Accordingly, they must be content to assent to the sensuous representations of scripture and to cling to the letter of the Law, submitting to its commandments and prohibitions without question. Ibn Ṭufayl's thesis is quite clear: the only language the masses are able to understand is the sensuous language of religious texts such as the Qur'an, which should be accepted literally.

Ibn Rushd

The greatest figure in the history of Andalusian philosophy, however, was unquestionably Abū'l-Walīd Muḥammad Ibn Aḥmad Ibn Rushd. Known in Latin as Averroes, he was born in Cordova in 1126. He studied Arabic letters, jurisprudence, *Kalām* and medicine with a number of teachers until the age of forty, when he was introduced to the Caliph Abū Ya'qūb Yūsuf who was an avid reader of Aristotelian texts, we are told by Ibn Ṭufayl, the Caliph's physician and counsellor. As a result of this introduction, the Caliph ordered Ibn Rushd to expound for him the works of Aristotle. As a keen reader of these works, he had found them 'intractable and abstruse'. At the same time Ibn Rushd was appointed religious judge (*qadi*) of Seville in 1169. In 1171, he was appointed chief judge of Cordova, and in 1182 royal physician at the court of Marakesh. When Abū Yūsuf

Ya'qūb, nicknamed al-Manṣūr, succeeded his father in 1184, the Caliph's patronage continued, but it appears that because of public pressure, the fortunes of Ibn Rushd took a sharp turn. He was exiled to Lucena to the south-east of Cordova in 1195, his books were publicly burned and the teaching of philosophy and the sciences, with the exception of medicine and astronomy, was banned. However, Ibn Rushd's exile did not last long; for, as we are told, the Caliph was soon 'reconciled to him and resumed his study of philosophy', of which he was fond. In 1198, Ibn Rushd died at the age of seventy-two.

Ibn Rushd's philosophical, medical and theological output was voluminous and matches the output of al-Fārābi and Ibn Sīna, his only two equals in the East. However, he outstrips them in three fundamental respects: his thoroughness in commenting on Aristotle or interpreting his thought, his contribution to jurisprudence (*fiqh*) in two important works (one of which has survived) and his very significant contribution to theology, or *Kalām*. In the first respect, Ibn Rushd wrote the most extensive commentaries on all the works of Aristotle with the exception of the *Politics*, which for some strange reason was not translated into Arabic until modern times. In the case of the *Physics*, the *Metaphysics*, *De anima*, *De coelo* and *Analytica posteriora*, Ibn Rushd actually wrote three types of commentary, known as the large, the intermediate and the short, to which should be added his paraphrase of Plato's *Republic*. This last work has survived in a Hebrew translation, whereas almost all the remaining works exist in Latin and a fair number of them in Arabic.

Ibn Rushd's more original writings in theology include *Tahāfut al-Tahāfut* (The Incoherence of the Incoherence), *Faṣ al-Maqāl* (The Decisive Treatise) and *al-Kashf 'an Manāhij al-Adillah* (The Exposition of the Methods of Proof). In the first of these writings, Ibn Rushd confronts al-Ghazāli's assault on philosophy head on, and in the process defines his own attitude to the major expositors of Aristotle's philosophy in the East, whom al-Ghazāli had singled out as the two targets of his assault, namely, al-Fārābi and Ibn Sīna. In the other two books, he launches a broader attack on Ash'arite theology. The pivotal issue on which those two works turn is the relation of philosophy and religion. For al-Kindi, as already mentioned, they were in perfect harmony, and for al-Fārābi and Ibn Sīna they were compatible to a limited extent. For al-Ghazāli, contrariwise, the differences between religion, i.e. Islam, and philosophy, i.e. Neoplatonism, were irreconcilable.

Ibn Rushd, who believed in what we may call the parity of truth, both philosophical and religious, was convinced that these differences were, indeed, reconcilable, if, as a first step, we were to comply with the Qur'anic injunction in Sūrah 3, 5–6, to discriminate clearly between those verses described as 'sound' (*muḥkamāt*) and those described as 'ambiguous' (*mutashābihāt*).

The questions on which the endless controversies between the theologians and the philosophers had turned, according to Ibn Rushd, actually centred on those 'ambiguous' verses of the Qur'an. The masses at large took them at their face value, and the Ash'arites interpreted them in a rigid manner which did not proceed far beyond the letter, as their theory of *bilā kayfa*, or comparative agnosticism, implied. The clue to resolving the conflicts arising from those controversies, according to Ibn Rushd, was to comply with the canons of interpretation (*ta'wīl*), as urged by the Qur'an and practised by the earliest Muslim scholars in matters of jurisprudence. As to the arbiters of interpretation, as applied now to the ambiguous verses of the Qur'an already referred to, Ibn Rushd was convinced, on the basis of his own reading of those verses referring to 'God and those firmly rooted in knowledge', that only the philosophers were the masters of genuine interpretation.[10]

Consider those verses of the Qur'an which, like 7, 54; 2, 27; and 10, 30, speak of God 'sitting upon the Throne', as an example. According to Ibn Rushd, the masses, referred to by him as the Literalists, take these verses at face value, whereas the Ash'arites, despite their qualified rationalism, do not proceed beyond those Literalists, and urge us to believe in their truth without question (*bilā kayfa*). The early jurists like Mālik Ibn Anas had taken this position; he regarded 'questioning' those Qur'anic passages, which speak of God sitting upon the Throne, as a heresy.[11]

At the root of the aversion to the use of the methods of interpretation, Ibn Rushd then observes, is the belief that it is affiliated to the use of deduction (*qiyās*) or syllogistic reasoning, which was 'invented' by foreign nations, i.e. the Greeks. Like al-Kindi, centuries earlier, Ibn Rushd takes up the cudgels against the preachers of such xenophobia, and asserts that, 'since philosophy is the study of existing entities, in so far as they are made; that is, in so far as they point to the Maker',[12] we are not only exhorted, but even urged in the Qur'an to 'reflect' upon existing entities, which is precisely the business of philosophy.[13] As for the arguments of the ancients bearing on these existing things, Ibn Rushd argues that our duty is to examine them carefully and judiciously. If we find that they accord with the 'conditions of sound demonstration', we should accept them, rejoice in them and thank them (i.e. the ancients) graciously. 'If not,' he goes on to argue, 'we should draw attention to them, warn against them and excuse them', since they have tried hard but failed.[14]

The *Tahāfut*, Ibn Rushd's rebuttal of al-Ghazāli's own *Tahāfut al Falāsifah* (The Incoherence of the Philosophers), discussed in chapter 5, is one of the great classics of philosophical–theological debate. In it, Ibn Rushd meticulously examines each one of al-Ghazāli's 'twenty questions' or strictures against the Muslim Peripatetic philosophers. Three of these, it will be recalled, were singled out by al-Ghazāli as particularly damning: the eternity of the world, the denial of God's knowledge of particulars and the resurrection of the body.

Ibn Rushd's strategy in rebutting al-Ghazāli's arguments is spelt out in his *Faṣl al-Maqāl*, written in 1180, possibly before *al-Tahāfut*, written in the same year. Here, he explains that the conflict between the philosophers and the theologians is purely verbal or semantic. For if we take the eternity of the world as an example, we will find that of the three categories of entities on which the conflict revolves, i.e. God, particular objects and the universe as a whole, both sides are in agreement regarding the status of the first and second, only disagreeing on the status of the third. Yet their disagreement is not so radical as to justify the charge of infidelity (*kufr*) levelled at the philosophers. For if we examine the thesis of Aristotle and his Muslim followers, we will find that, unlike God, the universe is not said by them to be eternal in the real sense, since this would entail that, like God, it is uncaused, which the philosophers deny. Nor is it temporal (*muḥdath*) in the real sense, for then it would be corruptible (*fāsid*). Ibn Rushd finds confirmation for this view in the Qur'an itself, which states in Sūrah 11, 7, that 'He created the heavens and the earth while His Throne was upon the water.' This verse implies that the Throne, the water and the time which measures their duration are eternal. Likewise, Qur'an 41, 10, which states that God, having created the world in six days, 'arose unto heaven which consisted of smoke', implies that the heavens were created from smoke. Accordingly, in neither case can the eternity of the world or creation out of nothing be said to be asserted in the Qur'an in an 'unambiguous' way, as the theologians, including al-Ghazāli, actually claim. They are, instead, open to interpretation. This interpretation, as already mentioned, is the business of the philosophers alone, because they alone are able to apply the method of logical demonstration (*burhān*) unlike the theologians and the masses at large, who are only able to apply the inferior methods of dialectic (*jadal*) or rhetoric (*khatābah*) respectively.

In both the *Tahāfut* and *al-Kashf* Ibn Rushd, then, examines thoroughly the tenuous way in which the Ash'arites in general and al-Ghazāli in particular tried to overcome the difficulties inherent in their notion of creation in time by God, who is eternal and therefore independent of the conditions of time. This raised the question of whether, in that process, His essence was not liable to change, which the theologians emphatically denied. To overcome this difficulty, they then contended that God had created the world in time by an act of 'eternal will', as al-Ghazāli explicitly stated in his *Tahāfut*. For Ibn Rushd, the concept of an eternal will causing the world to come into being in time is self-contradictory: it presupposes an infinite lapse of time, during which God was idle, and confuses two fundamental concepts, namely willing and doing (*fi'l*), which are entirely different. Now, the universe, whether eternal or temporal, is clearly the product of God's 'doing' which, in view of His omnipotence, does not allow for the least lapse or interval between the act of doing and the actual production of its object, in this case the world, which comes into being instantly at the behest of God. Therefore, Ibn Rushd argues, God cannot create the world in time unless He is in time, which the theologians themselves reject. If we review, then, the various views of producing (*ījād*) the world proposed by Aristotle, the Neoplatonists and the 'theologians belonging to the three religious communities which exist today', he writes in his *Tafsir mā Ba'd al-Ṭabī'ah* (Large Commentary on the *Metaphysics* of Aristotle), we will find that the view 'which is the least doubtful and the most accordant with existing reality' is that of Aristotle. According to that view, 'production' is the act of bringing matter and form together, or actualizing the potential, rather than creating something out of nothing, which is absurd. It follows that in bringing the form and matter of the world together, God is the Maker of the resulting compound, i.e. the world. This process of 'composition' or 'conjunction' (*tarkīb* or *ribāṭ*) may be supposed to be continuous or discontinuous; for Ibn Rushd, there can be no question that only 'continuous production' (*iḥdāth dā'im*), as he calls it in the *Tahāfut*, is worthy of the omnipotent and eternal Maker of the universe.[15]

As for God's knowledge of particulars, on which al-Ghazāli's second major criticism of the philosophers turned, Ibn Rushd explains that the philosophers do not deny that God knows the multitude of created particulars, but only that His mode of knowledge is analogous to ours. They maintain, instead, that God's knowledge is the *cause* of these particulars, whereas ours is the *effect* of the objects known (*ma'lūm*). In other words, in the very act of knowing them, God causes them to come into being, while our own knowledge is dependent upon their coming into being and is conditioned by it.

The third major criticism levelled by al-Ghazāli was the philosophers' denial of bodily resurrection. Here Ibn Rushd is content to give a 'methodological' answer. 'Resurrection', he writes, 'has been affirmed by the religious laws (*sharā'i'*) and has been proved demonstratively by the philosophers.'[16] Those philosophers are unanimous that humankind should comply with the religious teachings and precepts enunciated by the prophets, in so far as they prescribe virtuous actions and pious observances. Resurrection, with which the prospects of punishment and reward are bound up, is unquestionably one of those commendable precepts. The only difference between the philosophers and the theologians on this score is that the 'mode' of resurrection favoured by each group is different; the philosophers for their part favour 'spiritual resurrection (*ma'ād rūḥani*)', whereas the theologians favour bodily resurrection. With respect to the *fact* of resurrection, both groups are in agreement. The Qur'an itself has 'represented' in sensuous images the mode of resurrection and the punishments and rewards awaiting humankind in the Hereafter, in order to make them more readily intelligible to the masses who, unlike the philosophers, cannot comprehend abstract, spiritual language.

Al-Ghazāli's fourth major criticism, which does not justify

the charge of infidelity, but only heresy, turns on the philosophers' contention that the 'correlation' between so-called causes and so-called effects is necessary. This contention, according to al-Ghazāli, as we have already seen, is entirely gratuitous; God can effect His grand cosmic designs imperiously and miraculously and is not subject to any restraints, causal or other.

In his rebuttal, Ibn Rushd argues that the denial of causation is simply a sophistical gambit, in which 'one denies verbally what is in his heart'; in other words, without serious conviction. For no reasonable person can deny that every action must have an agent on the one hand, or that, on the other, existing entities possess certain natures or properties, which determine their very names and definitions, as well as the actions or operations peculiar to them.

Moreover, it is self-evident, Ibn Rushd argues in classic Aristotelian fashion, that the knowledge of existing entities is synonymous with the knowledge of their causes, and this in turn is synonymous with the very concept of reason; so that, as he puts it, 'he who repudiates causes has in fact repudiated knowledge'.[17]

Even at the theological level, the denial of necessary causation would militate against the concept of divine wisdom, which determines the order governing His creation; so that everything could then be imagined to happen entirely by chance, without the preordination of its wise Maker. Such denial would also militate against the very possibility of proving God's existence from the observation of the beauty and order of this creation.

Apart from this, the arguments for the existence of God proposed by the Ash'arites are logically tenuous, argues Ibn Rushd. Their most famous argument from creation in time (*ḥudūth*) rests on a premise that they cannot prove; namely, that the world is indeed created in time (*ḥādith*). To bolster this thesis, the Ash'arites argue that the world is made up of atoms and accidents, which are subject, like the world itself, to time;

but neither the existence of atoms or indivisible particles nor their alleged temporal character (*ḥudūth*) is demonstrably certain, but is subject to 'insoluble doubts'. Even the argument from the contingency (*jawāz*) of the world, which the great Ash'arite theologian al-Juwayni proposed, following the lead of Ibn Sīna, is untenable, because it presupposes that everything in the world is contingent or possible and *ipso facto* could be otherwise. But if this were the case, and 'if things did not have necessary causes which determine their existence in that manner proper to that kind of existing entity, then there is really no knowledge proper to the Wise Creator, as against others ... nor will there be any wisdom predicable of any maker, as against anyone who is not a maker (*ṣāni'*)',[18] even where human agents are concerned.

Having rejected the two classical arguments for the existence of God proposed by the theologians and Ibn Sīna himself; namely, the argument from the temporal creation of the world (*ḥudūth*) and that of contingency (*jawāz*), Ibn Rushd proceeds to develop the argument from 'divine providence' (*'ināyah*) and that from invention (*ikhtirā'*), 'to which the Gracious Book [the Qur'an] has called attention', as he puts it. According to the first proof, everything in the world has been created for the purpose of subserving the higher interests of humankind and the survival of humanity; and according to the second, everything which exists or comes into being is an 'invention' of God, as numerous Qur'anic verses clearly mention.[19]

In conclusion, we may note that despite his serious reservations concerning Ibn Sīna, his chief rival in the East, with respect to the theory of emanation, on the one hand, and the contingency of the universe, on the other, Ibn Rushd continued to accept a major tenet of Islamic Neoplatonism, i.e. conjunction with the Active Intellect. The ultimate destiny of the soul, according to him, consisted in its liberation from the bondage of the body, whereby it is able to rejoin the intelligible world. For Ibn Rushd it is through 'conjunction' with the Active Intellect, as Ibn Sīna and Ibn Bājjah argued, that the process of cognition is consummated and the 'possible' intellect, which is for him eternal, becomes actualized.[20]

The subsequent history of Averroism, both in Islam and Western Europe, is particularly instructive. Ibn Rushd was criticized and vilified in the East and came under devastating attack in the West at the hands of ecclesiastical authorities in Paris in 1270 and 1277, on a variety of charges, such as the eternity of the world, the unity of the intellect and the denial of divine providence. His Latin Averroist supporters, with Siger de Brabant (d. 1281) at their head, imputed to him, erroneously we believe, the so-called thesis of Double Truth, according to which a proposition may be true in philosophy, but false in theology, or vice versa. In 1277, his books were burned at the doorstep of the Sorbonne, less than a century after being publicly burned in 1195 in Cordova. Nothing has consecrated the international standing of Averroes in philosophical quarters better than the fact that his commentaries on Aristotle have survived in Latin translation, whereas only a small part of these commentaries has survived in the original Arabic. Many of these Latin translations have been reprinted in modern editions in Europe and America.

8

The progress of anti-rationalism and the onset of decline

Ibn Ḥazm and Ibn Taymiyah

Although al-Ghazālī's assault on philosophy in the eleventh century was devastating, he had retained the right of reason to arbitrate in theological controversies, and distinguished clearly between those parts of philosophy 'which clash with fundamental principles of religion' and those that did not, like logic, ethics and mathematics. The latter, he argued, could only be questioned by 'an ignorant friend of Islam who is worse than a learned enemy'. Despite al-Ghazālī's reservations, however, the gap between philosophy and theology continued to widen during the next three centuries and beyond. The new anti-rationalism took one of two forms:

1. return to the Ḥanbalite position which rejected all philosophical, and even theological, methods of discourse, and clung to the sacred text, literally interpreted;
2. acquiescence in mysticism or the Sufi path, which tried to circumvent those methods by recourse to the methods of direct communication with the Divine, either through contemplation or organic union, as we have seen.

With respect to theological reaction, Ibn Ḥazm (d. 1064), Ibn Taymiyah (d. 1328) and Ibn Qayyim al-Jawziyah (d. 1300) may be taken as the chief representatives of the Neo-Ḥanbalite position.

A leading figure in the history of Andalusian literature, ethics and historiography, Ibn Ḥazm was born in Cordova in 994 and died in 1064. He wrote *Ṭawq al-Ḥamāmah* (The Ring of the Dove), on the art of courtship, *Kitāb al-Akhlāq wa'l Siyar* (The Book of Ethics and Ways of Life), *al-Fiṣal* (The Discriminations on Fancies and Creeds), and finally *al-Ibṭāl* (The Book of Rebuttal), which is of primary interest to us. In this book, Ibn Ḥazm rejects out of hand all forms of deduction, analogy, opinion or imitation (*taqlīd*) which the various schools of theology or jurisprudence had used over the centuries in some form or other. Then, he proceeds to reject all theological methods of discourse, whether Mu'tazilite or Ash'arite, which turned on such questions as the nature of God, the composition of substances or accidents, free will and predestination, divine justice and the like. Of the various methods of proof, he only accepts sense-experience, self-evidence and the explicit statements of the Qur'an and the Hadith, which should be interpreted purely literally, according to him.

Ibn Taymiyah was born in Ḥarrān in 1262 and died in Damascus in 1328. Like Ibn Ḥazm, this scholar was vehement in his attack on philosophy, as well as theology (*Kalām*), and called with the utmost insistence for a return to the ways of 'the pious ancestors' (*al-salaf al-ṣāliḥ*). This call was destined to become the slogan of all so-called 'reformist' and fundamentalist movements in Muslim lands down to the present day.

The source of all religious truth, according to Ibn Taymiyah, is the Qur'an, supplemented by the Hadith and interpreted by the Companions of the Prophet (*Ṣaḥābah*) or their immediate Successors (*Tābi'ūn*). The authority of those early scholars, confirmed by the consensus (*ijmā'*), is infallible.[1] None of the successors of those two generations can lay claim to infallibility, as the centuries of controversy in theology, philosophy and mysticism actually demonstrate. Furthermore, since the Companions and the Successors have solved all the problems that might interest the Muslim community, any opinions or practices that have emerged subsequently should be declared innovations or heresies (*bid'ah*). Ibn Taymiyah assigns to the category of adepts of innovation or heresy almost all the theological or religious groups that emerged following the death of the Prophet; namely, the Khārijites, the Shī'ites, the Murji'ites, the Mu'tazilites and even the Ash'arites, whose theology had become identified by that time with Sunnite orthodoxy. 'For my part,' he writes, quoting Fakhr al-Dīn al-Rāzi, 'I have examined all the theological methods and found them incapable of curing any ill or quenching any thirst. For me the best method is that of the Qur'an; in the affirmative, I read "The Merciful sat upon the Throne" [Qur'an 7, 52] ... in the negative, "Nothing is like unto Him" [Qur'an 42, 11].' The philosophers, he goes on to assert, just as much as the theologians, have been unable to prove the justice, mercy or wisdom of God, or even His truthfulness, and have been at loggerheads with each other, chiefly because they have departed from the tradition of the ancestors (*al-salaf*).[2]

Ibn Taymiyah's attack on the philosophers is particularly scathing. The substance of their teaching, he observes, is that revealed scriptures, including the Qur'an, are primarily addressed to the masses at large, and are couched in pictorial language accessible to them; but religious propositions or articles of faith are not necessarily true. They serve at best a social purpose by inculcating virtuous conduct and pious observances, as Ibn Rushd had actually argued.

In *al-'Aql wa'l-Naql* (The Harmony of Reason and Tradition), Ibn Taymiyah attacks Ibn Rushd for limiting the number of theological groups in *al-Kashf* to four: the esoterics, the literalists, the Mu'tazilites and the Ash'arites; to the exclusion of the 'pious ancestors' (*salaf*), 'whose creed', he writes, 'is the best creed of this [Muslim] community till the Day of Resurrection'. Then, contrary to his anti-philosophical pretensions, he proceeds to examine the arguments of Ibn Rushd one by one and to refute them philosophically.[3]

More significant, perhaps, is his critique in *al-Radd 'ala'l Manṭiqiyīn* (The Refutation of the Logicians) of the basic tenets of Aristotelian logic. First, the Aristotelian theory of definition is untenable, because of the difficulty of determining the so-called *infima species* and the 'essential differentiae' upon which definition really depends. Second, the Aristotelian theory of the syllogism is equally untenable, because the philosophers divide judgements upon which the syllogism rests into self-evident or not self-evident; but considering the great diversity of mental aptitudes, the ability to grasp the middle term, upon which the possibility of syllogistic reasoning actually depends, will vary a great deal and so will the validity of logical reasoning, which becomes thereby doubly subjective and relative.

The highest form of reasoning, according to the logicians, is demonstration (*burhān*); but even if we grant the validity of demonstration, we are forced to admit that its conclusions are vacuous. For demonstration, as such, bears on universals which exist in the mind; whereas the beings to which they are supposed to correspond are particulars, which exist in fact; so that demonstration will not yield any positive knowledge of particular entities, or even of God.

Finally, the philosophers recognize five kinds of substances; form, matter, body, soul and intellect, as well as ten categories. Now, these two lists have not been shown to be exhaustive, and do not apply, at any rate, to the highest entities, such as God and the 'separate entities', or contribute in the least to our knowledge of those higher entities.[4]

Ibn Taymiyah's best-known disciple was Ibn Qayyim al-Jawziyah, another key figure in the history of reaction against philosophy, theology and mysticism. The revival of Ḥanbalism, of which those two scholars were the staunchest advocates in the fourteenth century, culminated in the rise of the Wahhābi movement, founded in the eighteenth century by Muḥammad Ibn 'Abd al-Wahhāb (d. 1792). It became the official creed of the Sa'udi dynasty, following that dynasty's success in establishing its hegemony in Najd and Hijāz. The Wahhābis share with Ibn Taymiyah and his school, in addition to adherence to the Qur'an, literally interpreted, and the Hadith as a supplement thereof, strict observance of the Muslim rituals and the condemnation of the cult of saints and similar excesses of the Sufi orders.

Fakhr al-Dīn al-Rāzi and his successors

During the twelfth and thirteenth centuries, theological developments continued on a much broader front. The extreme literalism and traditionalism of Ibn Ḥazm and Ibn Taymiyah was challenged or moderated by a number of theologians, the most important of whom during the twelfth century was Fakhr al-Dīn al-Rāzi. His moderation was pursued during the next three centuries by a group of less well-known authors who will be discussed here.

Born in Rayy in 1149, Fakhr al-Dīn al-Rāzi travelled extensively throughout Persia, enjoyed the patronage of the Ghaznawid Sultans and died in Herat in 1209. His major philosophical works include a commentary on Ibn Sīnā's *Ishārāt* and *'Uyūn al-Ḥikmah*, together with his massive *al-Mabāḥith al-Mashriqiyah* (Oriental Investigations). His theological writings include *al-Arbā'īn fī Uṣūl al-Dīn* (The Forty [Questions] of Religious Principles) and *al-Muḥaṣṣal* (Acquisition), to which may be added his voluminous commentary on the Qur'an, *Mafātīh al-Ghayb* (Keys of the Mystery). The chief merit of these writings, as Ibn Khaldūn was to observe later, is that their author has fully exploited in them the methods of the philosophers, in his rebuttal of those propositions that he believed to be in conflict with Islamic doctrine. Unlike al-Ghazāli, al-Rāzi hardly recognizes any conflict between philosophy and theology and is willing to combine them in an artful manner. His debt to Ibn Sīna in this respect is considerable; and even when he poses as his critic, his dependence on that seminal philosopher is transparent. For instance, in *al-Mabāḥith* he develops a theory of essence and existence which is thoroughly Avicennian, and according to which the concept of essence does not entail existence, nor does a property of the former necessarily apply to the other. It follows that the essence requires an extraneous determination to cause it to exist, and this determination is due to the Necessary Being.[5] However, he rejects Ibn Sīna's emanationist view, as well as the maxim that out of the One only one entity can arise. For him, the First Being gives rise to the first intellect, which already involves an element of plurality by virtue of its dual character as possible in itself and necessary due to its Cause, and this is how plurality finds its way into the universe as a whole. Equally, he is more explicit than Ibn Sīna in his account of God's knowledge of particulars; according to him, God knows Himself as the Cause of all things and in the process comes to know all created entities, of which He is the Cause. This divine knowledge, contrary to Ibn Sīna's claims, does not entail plurality, change or dependence on its mutable objects. The reason given by al-Rāzi is that knowledge is not the act of assimilating the form of the knowable, as the Neoplatonists, including Ibn Sīna, claim, but is rather a special relation of the knower to the object known, which does not affect or alter the knower in any way.[6]

As for human cognition in general, al-Rāzi describes it as a form of illumination, issuing ultimately from the 'world of emanation', or the intelligible world, once the soul has become disposed for its reception. Sensation plays simply the incidental role of preparing the soul for this reception. The primary principles of cognition, however, are known intuitively and they are the foundation of all knowledge.

In the field of epistemology, al-Rāzi, like Avicenna, rejects the Platonic theory of recollection, according to which the soul simply recalls or remembers those intelligibles with which it was originally conversant, but had forgotten upon its descent into the body. For both al-Rāzi and Avicenna, this theory of cognition is untenable, in so far as the soul, far from having pre-existed in a world of its own, i.e. Plato's World of Ideas, was created in time and could not possibly, for that reason, have any knowledge preceding its creation.

As for God's knowledge of particulars; which set the philosophers and theologians (*mutakallimūn*) at loggerheads ever since al-Ghazāli had launched his famous onslaught on the Muslim Neoplatonists, with Avicenna at their head; al-Rāzi takes an anti-Avicennian stand too. This stand has a certain similarity to that of his Arab-Spanish contemporary, Averroes (d. 1198), with whose works he was probably not familiar. The gist of al-Rāzi's view of God's knowledge is that, through the same act of self-knowledge whereby he knows Himself as the cause of all created entities; particular or universal, God knows the whole of the created order. Against the Avicennian charge that God's knowledge of particulars entails plurality in His essence, al-Rāzi argues that knowledge is not a process of assimilating or apprehending the form of the knowable, as Avicenna and the Neoplatonists hold, but rather a special relationship to the object known. What changes in the process of God's knowledge of particulars is not God's essence, but rather his relationship to that object. Accordingly, both on his authority and that of Abu'l-Barakāt al-Baghdādi, which he invokes in support of his own view, al-Rāzi reaffirms the all-embracing character of God's knowledge of Himself as well as all created entities, universal or particular. He succeeds in that respect by rebutting the charge of al-Ghazāli, that in denying God's knowledge of particulars, the philosophers had in fact reduced Him to the status of the dead or the ignorant, without subscribing to Avicenna's tenuous view that God knows particulars in a universal way, or that He has a purely universal knowledge of the world.

Be this as it may, al-Rāzi stands out as a key figure in the development of Islamic thought in the post-Avicennian period, both in the encyclopedic range of his learning and his philosophical acumen. In addition, better than any of his contemporaries in the East, he tried valiantly, but with a great deal of prolixity and repetitiousness, to bring into some kind of harmony the antithetic position of the philosophers and the theologians (*mutakallimūn*) of Islam.

Subsequent developments in theology continued the tradition of anti-philosophical discourse initiated by al-Ghazāli. The thirteenth century, in addition, marked the beginning of a period of decline, during which theological output was limited to the writing of commentaries or super-commentaries on the works of classical authors. The noteworthy theologians of the thirteenth and fourteenth centuries include Ḥāfiẓ al-Dīn al-Nasafi (d. 1301 or 1310); 'Aḍud al-Dīn al-Ījī (d. 1355), author of *al-Mawāqif*; and al-Taftazāni (d. 1390), who is best known for his commentary on the *'Aqidah* (Creed) of Najm al-Dīn al-Nasafi (d. 1142). This *Creed* remained for centuries one of the standard textbooks in theology. Mention must also be made of al-Sharif al-Jurjani (d. 1413), best known for his commentary on al-Īji's *al-Mawāqif* and his famous glossary of technical terms, known as *al-Ta'rifāt*. The most important theologians of the fifteenth century are al-Sanūsi (d. *c.*1490) and al-Dawwāni (d. 1501), author of a well-known treatise on ethics, written in Persian. The authors who contributed to theological commentary or exposition after the fifteenth century are al-Birqili (d. 1570); al-Laqani (d. 1621), author of *Jawharat al-Tawḥīd* (The Jewel of Unity), which became the subject of numerous commentaries or glossaries; al-Sialkūti (d. 1657); and al-Bājuri

(d. 1860), author of a commentary on al-Laqani's *Jawharah*. In the nineteenth century, Muḥammad 'Abduh (d. 1905) emerged as the chief exponent of Islamic theology in his *Risālat al-Tawḥid* (Epistle of Unity) (see chapter 10).

Ibn Khaldūn of Tunis and his new philosophy of history

'Abd al-Raḥmān Ibn Khaldūn was born in Tunis in 1332 and studied the religious and linguistic sciences with a number of teachers, for whom he had the highest regard. In 1352, he travelled west and settled down in Fez. He then went east to Alexandria and Cairo, where he met the Mamlūk Sultan al-Ẓāhir Barqūq, who appointed him professor of Māliki jurisprudence, then chief *qadi* of Egypt. Towards the end of his life, in 1401, we are told in his autobiography, he met Timurlane outside the walls of Damascus. The Mongol conqueror received the scholar very well and expressed his desire to attach him to his service, but Ibn Khaldūn chose to return to Cairo to continue his work as *qadi* and writer till his death in 1406.

One of the last great figures in the history of Islamic thought, Ibn Khaldūn occupies a dual position in that history. He was both a compiler of the Islamic sciences and letters, as well as philosophy and Sufism, in his famous *Muqaddimah* (Prolegomena) to his universal history, and the author of the first and only philosophy of history in Islam.

To begin with, Ibn Khaldūn divides the sciences into rational, traditional and linguistic, in a manner reminiscent of al-Fārābi and his *Iḥṣā' al-'Ulum* (Enumeration of the Sciences). The first division, which he calls natural, includes the philosophical sciences such as logic, physics, mathematics and metaphysics, whereas the second includes the religious sciences grounded in the Qur'an and Hadith, such as the science of exegesis (*tafsīr*), transmission of Hadith, jurisprudence and *Kalām*. The linguistic sciences include philology, grammar, rhetoric and literature (*adab*).[7]

Although Ibn Khaldūn regards the philosophical sciences as perfectly natural, 'having existed in the human race since the birth of civilization', he is highly critical of them, because of 'the great damage they can cause one's religion', as he puts it. In his detailed critique of the philosophical sciences, he begins by noting that the philosophers claim that the knowledge of sensible and super-sensible objects alike is possible through philosophical speculation and logical deduction; even religious beliefs, they contend, can be known through reason, rather than revelation (*sam'*). Their starting-point is that universal notions or general concepts are derived from particulars of sense through the process of abstraction, culminating in the simplest and most universal of these notions called by them the highest genera, i.e. the categories. They then go on to argue that demonstration consists in the combination of these notions, either affirmatively or negatively. From this combination, according to them, perfect conception arises; and this is the ultimate goal of the 'cognitive quest'. Human happiness, they believe, consists in apprehending sensible and super-sensible realities through logical proof, leading up to 'conjunction' with the Active Intellect.

In his critique, Ibn Khaldūn first observes that in the physical sciences, the claims of the philosophers are unwarranted, because their demonstrations are incapable of proving the complete correspondence between their 'conceptual conclusions' and the natural objects they are supposed to apply to, as Ibn Taymiyah had already observed. For those conclusions are purely conceptual and universal, whereas natural objects are concrete and particular. Add to this that engaging in this type of enquiry is sinful, 'because questions of physics do not concern us, either in our religion or our livelihood, and therefore we should abandon them'.[8]

If we consider, next, entities lying outside the realm of sense, i.e. spiritual entities on which metaphysics turns, we will find, according to Ibn Khaldūn, that these entities 'are entirely unknowable and can never be attained or demonstrated'; our only means of proving their existence is the inner sense, through which we apprehend our own selves. He then quotes Plato as saying: 'In metaphysics, it is not possible to attain reality [Arabic, *ainen*, for Greek, *einai*, to be]; we can only speak thereof in terms of what is more fitting or more likely, meaning opinion (*ẓann*, *doxa*).' If so, comments Ibn Khaldūn, and 'if we can attain nothing more than opinion after much hardship and toil, we had better be content with the opinion that we had in the first place'.[9]

Moreover, if we take the philosophers' concept of happiness, as lying in 'conjunction' with the Active Intellect, we will find that it is inadequate, since it is purely intellectual, resembling in some respects the ecstasy of which the Sufis speak. However, this condition is attainable, according to the Sufis, by the practice of the mystical way and the mortification of the self, not rational deductions rooted in 'bodily cognitions'. Genuine spiritual cognitions are only possible for the soul, which is able to apprehend itself directly, without any intermediaries; but even these apprehensions are possible, only 'if the veil of sense is lifted'.[10]

Despite all these serious strictures, Ibn Khaldūn does not deny that philosophy has at least one positive advantage: it sharpens the mind and enables us to formulate arguments in accordance with the rules of logic. However, it is fraught with dangers; therefore 'let him who dabbles in it do so after mastering religious subjects and acquainting himself with the sciences of exegesis (*tafsīr*) and jurisprudence.'[11]

The positive contribution of Ibn Khaldūn lies in his elaboration of a 'science of civilization', with hardly a precedent in Arab-Islamic thought, as well as a philosophy of history grounded in the dialectic of social development or transformation. The starting-point of this science of civilization is the Aristotelian maxim that the individual is by nature a social animal, since individuals cannot provide for their essential needs or protect themselves against external aggression without the assistance of their fellows. It is for this reason that human association requires a ruler or king who is able to deter aggression. The office of such a ruler, or kingship, is either natural and ultimately rooted in conquest and the spirit of solidarity (*'aṣabiyah*) or it is religious and rooted in religious ordinances or provisions. Of the two polities, the natural (designated as rational by Ibn Khaldūn) and the religious, the latter is definitely superior because it attends to people's dual happiness in this world and in the world to come, while the former attends to their earthly happiness only.

As for the forms of human association, they vary according to climatic, geographic and economic factors, which have a decisive influence on people's humours or temperament. That is why, according to Ibn Khaldūn, we find that the inhabitants of the torrid zone, such as the Sudanese or Egyptians, are more prone to levity, merriment and distraction, unlike the inhabitants of the frigid zones, who tend to be more melancholy, reserved and concerned about the morrow. These ecological factors and the resultant temperamental variations determine, ultimately, the kind of association involved and the laws of its development. Of these forms of human association, the nomadic and the sedentary are the two principal kinds on which Ibn Khaldūn's philosophy of history actually turns.

The nomadic mode of life, he explains, is marked by virility, fitness and aggressiveness; whereas the sedentary or urban is marked by passivity, dullness and indolence. In these conditions, it is inevitable that, sooner or later, the inhabitants of the city (*ḥadar*) should be so weakened by the vices of city life as to lose the stamina and ruggedness that desert life breeds in the nomads (*badw*, bedouin), whereupon they fall an easy prey to the latter. Once those denizens of the desert have changed roles with their victims, they are gradually exposed to the vices of city life, and accordingly fall prey, in turn, to a new wave of nomadic invaders.

Ibn Khaldūn dwells at length on this nomadic–sedentary, sedentary–nomadic cycle and has worked out in detail the stages through which society or the state passes before its final collapse. Those stages correspond to the 'ages' through which each such state must pass. The 'natural age' of the state, according to him, is equivalent to three generations of forty years each, which is the natural age of a person. As one would expect, the first generation is characterized by the ruggedness of desert life and the ardour of the spirit of tribal solidarity; the second by the weakening of that spirit as a result of the transition to a mode of sedentary or city life; and the third by the total loss of the spirit of solidarity. When this happens, the days of the state are numbered and are finally sealed by 'God's decree to bring about its final dissolution'.

In more specific terms, the state or political community that comes into being once the nomads have settled down to an urban mode of life passes through five stages, reflecting the pattern of its evolution or transformation.

1. The first is the stage of conquest, during which the authority of the ruler or king rests on a solid foundation of readiness to defend the state against external aggression and to participate in government, as the spirit of tribal solidarity stipulates.
2. The second is the stage of despotism, during which the ruler begins to monopolize power and exclude his own tribesmen, and to depend instead on foreign troops or mercenaries for defending his office. As a result, the spirit of solidarity begins to wane and strife or discord begins to replace the collective sense of cohesion and mutual support.

3. The third is the stage of leisure and stability, during which the ruler proceeds to enjoy the fruits of success, levies taxes and engages in the construction of public buildings, monuments and temples, in an attempt to vie with foreign rulers.
4. The fourth is the stage of contentment and pacification, during which the ruler is content to continue in the footsteps of his predecessors without attempting to introduce any changes.
5. The fifth is the stage of extravagance, during which the ruler squanders the public treasure on his pleasures and those of his retainers. Thereupon, the state begins to disintegrate and the supporters and retainers of the ruler begin to disperse. The state is so weakened at this point that it falls an easy prey to a new wave of nomadic invaders.

Ibn Khaldūn's philosophy of history, exhibited in this cyclical theory of the state and the inevitable transition from a nomadic to a sedentary or urban life, rests on two parallel lines of determinism, emanating from the divine Decree, on the one hand, and the pressure of geographic and ecological forces, on the other. Even worthiness to assume political office, or wresting it from other rulers, depends on the divine Decree. For the very existence of 'polities and kingships', writes Ibn Khaldūn,

> is the warrant of mankind's survival and of God's assignment of vicegerency (*khilāfah*) to some of His servants, so as to carry out His ordinances. For God's ordinances are laid upon His creatures and servants with a view to their good and welfare ... unlike human ordinances which stem from ignorance and are the work of the Devil, in contradistinction to the power of God Almighty and His Decree. For, He is the Doer of both good and evil and is their Determiner, since there is no other doer (*fā'il*) than He.[12]

There is in this concluding statement, which is thoroughly reminiscent of al-Ghazāli, who was equally committed to the view that God is the Sole Agent in the universe, a hint of mysticism to which Ibn Khaldūn inclined, despite the positivist and empiricist outlook on which he built his sociology and his philosophy of history. In fact, among Ibn Khaldūn's extant works a mystical treatise, *Shifā' al-Sā'il*, reveals his profound Sufi sympathies in a perfectly explicit way.

9

Illuminationism (*Ishrāq*) and the reconciliation of Neoplatonism and Sufism

Al-Suhrawardi

We have referred in chapter 4 to Ibn Sīna's disenchantment in some of his later works with conventional Neoplatonism or Peripatetism (*Mashshā'iyah*), as he calls it, and his claim to have developed in his 'Oriental Wisdom' a more original and personal philosophy, into which certain oriental elements have been incorporated. The *Oriental Wisdom* has not reached us in the form described by Ibn Sīna, but in *al-Ishārat wa'l Tanbihāt* (Indications and Admonitions), one of his later works, as well as the short 'mystical' epistles of *The Bird*, *Love* and *Ḥayy Ibn Yaqẓān*, a clear tendency to bypass conjunction (*ittiṣāl*) in the direction of mystical union (*ittiḥād*) is discernible. However, the philosopher with whose name the 'Oriental Wisdom' or illumination (*ishrāq*) is associated is Shihāb al-Dīn al-Suhrawardi. He was born in Aleppo, Syria, in 1154 and was killed by order of Saladin in 1191, on the undefined charge of blasphemy and in response to the pressure of theologians and jurists. Like Ibn Sīna, al-Suhrawardi claimed that his aim in a number of his treatises was to expound his views in accordance with the conventional Peripatetic method. This he describes as a 'good discursive method' that is not adequate, however, to the aims of the 'godly sage' (*muta'allih*) who aspires to attain the rank of 'experiential wisdom', or that of both discursive and experiential methods combined. This latter task, he claims, was accomplished in his best-known work, entitled the *Ḥikmah al-Ishrāq* (The Wisdom of Illumination). As a prelude to the exposition of this wisdom, he explains in another work, *al-Talwiḥāt*, that the Peripatetics of his day have failed to understand the intent of its founder, Aristotle, the 'First Teacher and Master of Wisdom', as he calls him. Aristotle, we are told, appeared to al-Suhrawardi in a dream; whereupon al-Suhrawardi engaged him in a discussion of the nature of knowledge, conjunction and union, as well as the status of the philosophers of Islam and the Sufis, who had attained the level of 'concrete knowledge and visual contact', and were accordingly the true philosophers and sages. What distinguished those Sufi sages, according to al-Suhrawardi, was the fact that they had partaken of an 'ancient wisdom', which had remained unchanged despite the many forms, Aristotelian, Platonic, Greek or Persian, it had taken over the centuries. Its roots went back to Plato, the 'Master of Wisdom' and its head, and beyond him to Hermes and the other great sages like Empedocles and Pythagoras. This wisdom, based on the oriental dualism of light and darkness, was in fact the legacy of the Persian sages such as Jamasp, Frashaustra, Bizrgimher and their predecessors, according to al-Suhrawardi. It had had its Western representatives, including Plato, Agathodaimon and Ascelepius, followed by al-Bisṭāmi and al-Ḥallāj and had culminated in al-Suhrawardi himself.[1]

The core of the 'wisdom of illumination', for al-Suhrawardi, is the 'science of light', which deals with the nature of light and the manner of its diffusion. This light, according to him, is indefinable, because it is the most manifest reality; it is indeed the reality which 'manifests' all other things and is the substance that enters into the composition of all other substances, material or immaterial. Everything other than 'Pure Light', he goes on to explain, consists either of that which requires a bearer, and is called the 'dark substance', or the form of that substance, which is darkness itself. Material objects, in so far as they are capable of receiving both light and darkness, are called isthmuses (singular, *barzakh*), which, in themselves, are pure darkness and receive all the light permeating them from an outside source.[2]

As for its relation to objects beneath it, light is of two kinds, light in and for itself and light in and for another. It is this latter light that illuminates all things; but whether in itself or in another, light is supremely manifest, as already mentioned, and is the cause of the manifestation of all things which actually emanate from it. It follows, therefore, that it is living, since life is nothing but the essential self-manifestation outwardly in other things.

At the top of the scale of being stand the pure lights, which form an ascending ladder whose climactic point is the Light of Lights, upon which the existence of all the lights beneath it, whether pure or composite, depends. In that sense, this light is identical with the Necessary Being of Ibn Sīna; for the series of lights must terminate in a First or Necessary Light which is the source of all light and which al-Suhrawardi calls invariably the Self-Subsisting Light, the Holy Light, the Necessary Being and so on.

In addition to necessity, the Light of Lights is characterized by unity. For if we posit two primary lights, we would be involved in this contradiction, that they must derive their being from a third light, which is entirely one. Similarly, it is characterized by the capacity to impart its light to all the secondary lights emanating from it. The first of these lights is called by al-Suhrawardi the First Light, which differs from its source or the Light of Lights only in the degree of its perfection or purity.

Next, from the First Light emanate the secondary lights, the heavenly bodies and the physical compounds or elements making up the physical world, to which al-Suhrawardi applies the name 'isthmuses'. This latter world may also be described as the shadow of the Light of Lights or its penumbra and, like its source or cause, is eternal. Al-Suhrawardi, then, advances a series of arguments that are essentially Aristotelian in form, to prove the eternity of the world on the basis of the eternity of motion. From this he concludes that the world is an eternal emanation from its first principle, or the Light of Lights.

Physical objects, according to al-Suhrawardi, arise as a result of the combination of 'contrary natures', the predominant element in these objects being that light which is called Isfandar Mood, whose talisman is earth or dust. From the most perfect mode of elemental combinations arise humans, who receive their perfection from the angel Gabriel. This is the Holy Spirit, which breathes into humankind the human spirit, called the 'Isfahbad of humanity'. However, in addition to the 'human light' or rational soul, there dwell in the human body two powers, the irascible, which is manifested in conquest, and the desiderative, which is manifested in love.[3] As for the subsidiary faculties of nutrition and reproduction, they result from the diverse relationships between the body and light, and may be described as the various manifestations of the terrestrial light. In its management of the body, the terrestrial light takes the form of spirit (*rūḥ*), located in the left ventricle of the heart. This spirit permeates the whole body and transmits to its organs the light which it receives from the terrestrial light. However, the great diversity of bodily functions does not require a corresponding diversity of organs; accordingly the three internal faculties of *sensus communis*, imagination and estimation (*wahm*), contrary to Ibn Sīna's view, are one in genus, since they all derive from the terrestrial light, which perceives sensible objects by means of bodily organs. For that reason they may be called 'the sense of senses'.

The conjunction of the terrestrial light with matter is the outcome of its conjunction with the dark powers of the lower world; that is why it remains a stranger in this world and dwells grudgingly in the human body. It dwells at first in the lower animals and then ascends into the higher animals. This upward movement cannot be reversed, contrary to the theory of transmigration propounded by Plato and Pythagoras, which allows for a downward movement of the soul, or its reincarnation in the bodies of lower animals. Al-Suhrawardi is ambivalent with respect to that theory and appears to concede its major presupposition, i.e. the ultimate return of the soul to its original abode in the intelligible world. For him, the final liberation of the terrestrial light from the bondage of the body in which it dwells and which it manages is contingent upon the disintegration of the body. Transmigration is not a necessary condition of that liberation, since the light imprisoned in the body will be able to rejoin the higher world of light to the extent it yearns for this world. Thereupon, it will be released from all the fetters which held it down and will be able to join the ranks of the 'holy spirits' which dwell in the world of pure light.[4]

Al-Shirāzi (Mulla Ṣadra) and his successors

The Ishrāqi tradition inaugurated by al-Suhrawardi became before long the distinctive mark of the Persian philosophical tradition. As philosophy entered upon a recessive course in the Middle East in the wake of al-Ghazāli's onslaught and the Mongol conquest of Baghdad about a century and a half later, it received fresh impetus in Persia, especially during the Safawid period. Shāh Ismā'il (1500–24), who claimed descent from a Sufi family, undertook to propagate the Shī'ite creed throughout Persia, with the consequent revival of theological and philosophical studies, which flourished during the reign of Shāh 'Abbās (1588–1629). A number of scholars distinguished themselves during this period. We might mention Mīr Dāmād (d. 1631) and Bahā' al-Dīn al-'Āmili (d. 1621), two of the teachers of Ṣadr al-Dīn al-Shirāzi (d. 1641), generally regarded as the greatest philosopher of modern Persia, where he is better known as Mulla Ṣadra.

Al-Shirāzi was born in Shirāz in 1572, then moved to Isfahān, an important centre of learning at that time. He studied there with Mīr Dāmād and Mīr Abū'l-Qāsim Findereski (d. 1640), then returned to Shirāz to assume a teaching position at a religious institution in that city. He is said to have performed the pilgrimage to Makkah on foot seven times, and died in Basrah on his way back from his seventh pilgrimage in 1641.

Al-Shirāzi's philosophical output was voluminous. He wrote commentaries on al-Suhrawardi's *Ḥikmat al-Ishrāq*, al-Abhari's *al-Hidāyah fi'l-Ḥikmah* and Ibn Sīna's *al-Shifā'*, in addition to original treatises on *Origination*, *Resurrection*, *Predicating Essence of Existence* and similar short tracts. His major philosophical works, however, are *al-Mashā'ir* (Apprehensions), *Kasr Asnām al-Jāhiliyah* (Breaking the Idols of Paganism) and 'Transcendental Wisdom', better known as 'The Four Journeys' (*al-Asfār al-Arba'ah*).

In *al-Asfār*'s opening parts, al-Shirāzi deplores the public's turning away from the study of philosophy, although the principles of philosophy coupled with the truths revealed to the prophets represent the highest expression of truth. He voices his conviction in the perfect harmony of philosophy and religion, which exhibit, according to him, a single truth which goes back to Adam. From Adam, this truth was transmitted to Abraham, then the Greek philosophers, then the Muslim mystics or Sufis and finally the common run of philosophers. The Greeks, he states, were originally star-worshippers, but in due course took over philosophy and theology from Abraham. He distinguishes in this context between two categories of ancient Greek philosophers. The first category starts with Thales and ends with Socrates and Plato; the second starts with Pythagoras, who received wisdom from Solomon and from the Egyptian priests, as reported in most Arabic histories of philosophy. Among the 'pillars of wisdom', al-Shirāzi mentions Empedocles, Pythagoras, Socrates, Plato and Aristotle. As for Plotinus, whom he calls the Greek Sage, he is often mentioned with appreciation, but on his relation to Plato and Aristotle, whose philosophies he so ably synthesized, al-Shirāzi, like the rest of the Muslim philosophers, is completely silent. All the above-mentioned Greek 'pillars of wisdom' are said by al-Shirāzi to have received the 'light of wisdom' from the 'beacon of prophethood', which is why they are in total agreement on such questions as the unity of God, the creation of the world and the resurrection.[5]

Apart from this account of philosophical history, a noteworthy feature of al-Shirāzi's methodology is the application of philosophical and Sufi categories to Shī'ism. He argues that the prophetic stage in world history came to an end with the death of Prophet Muḥammad, the 'Seal of the Prophets'. The Imamite or 'executor' stage (*wilāyah/wiṣāyah*) was then initiated by the twelve Shī'ite Imams; this will continue until the return of the twelfth Imam, who is in temporary concealment, according to Shī'ite doctrine. Al-Shirāzi, however, comments that in fact the 'executor' stage started with the prophet Sheth, who was to Adam what 'Ali was to Muḥammad, that is, successor or executor.[6] Al-Shirāzi finds a philosophical and mystical basis for this view in Ibn 'Arabi's concept of the 'Muḥammadan truth' or the divine Logos (*kalimah*), of which Muḥammad was the final and perfect manifestation. Like Ibn 'Arabi, al-Shirāzi, too, believed that this truth had two aspects, an overt and a covert one, and since Muḥammad himself was the manifestation of 'prophetic truth', then 'Ali, the first Imam, and his successors were all manifestations of the 'successor truth'. When the Mahdi or

Awaited Imam appears at the end of time, the whole meaning of revelation will be fully exhibited, and humankind will return to the pure monotheistic creed which Abraham was the first to proclaim and Muḥammad the last to confirm.

The four journeys of the soul, as given in *al-Asfār al-Arba'ah*, are:

1. from the creation (*khalq*) to the True Reality (*Ḥaqq*);
2. through the True Reality to the True Reality;
3. from the True Reality to creation, through the True Reality;
4. in creation through the True Reality.

The first part of al-Shirāzi's *magnum opus* deals with metaphysical questions of the type Ibn Sīna dealt with, his starting-point being the Avicennian thesis that existence has no *differentia* or species and is accordingly indefinable. It differs from essence merely conceptually; from this statement al-Shirāzi infers that the object of divine creation is not essence, as al-Suhrawardi and al-Dawwāni had argued, but rather existence, in so far as it is predicable of essence.[7] It follows that essence is an antecedent form of existence, if not in itself, then in relation to the divine act of creation. Thus, al-Shirāzi considers the realm of essences as equivalent to that of the 'fixed entities' of Ibn 'Arabi, which are the universal forms or archetypes according to which the world was fashioned, as Plato had originally proposed.

The dualism of essence and existence, he goes on to argue, is a characteristic of created entities of which the Necessary Being is entirely free. He imparts to every created entity its specific mode of existence by way of radiation or illumination (*ishrāq*). This Necessary Being is synonymous with the Light of Lights and may be described, therefore, as the source or fount from which material entities derive their luminous character and their resemblance to the Necessary Being. What sets them apart, however, is their essentially dark nature, whereby they are thoroughly different from the Light of Lights.

In the metaphysical parts of *al-Asfār*, al-Shirāzi is continually struggling to bring together Avicennian, Ishrāqi and Sufi elements. To begin with, he endorses Avicenna's theory of motion and maintains, along essentially Aristotelian lines, that this motion is ultimately dependent on a first Unmoved Mover, or God. He does not seem to be aware of the adverse implications of this theory of motion for his creationist thesis, which he advances as an alternative to Avicennian emanationism.

Light of Lights
(Necessary Being)
|
World of Command or Fixed Entities
(intelligible world)
|
Intelligible Forms
(human souls)
|
Universal Sphere
(Outermost sphere)
|
World of Creation
(material world)

Notwithstanding this, he appears to be inclined to endorse some aspects of emanationism by fitting them into an Ishraqi framework. Thus, like Ibn 'Arabi, he distinguishes in the Supreme Reality (*al-Ḥaqq*), the aspect of unity or Godhead, which the Sufis call the Blindness (*al-'Amā'*) or the Mystery (*al-Ghayb*), and the subordinate manifestations of this Reality, which Ibn 'Arabi called the 'fixed entities', but al-Shirazi calls 'possible essences'. Those possible essences have, according to him, two aspects: one whereby they are necessary in relation to their Cause, and another whereby they fall short of this perfection and form so many subordinate rungs on the ladder of created existence. This double relation of created being, whereby it is necessary through its Cause, but possible in itself, is a well-known aspect of Avicenna's attempt to explain the relation of the contingent universe to its Necessary Cause or the Necessary Being, as he calls it.

However, the possible essences represent in a sense the first mode of diversification of the Supreme Reality, as Ibn Arabi has also taught in his attempt to safeguard the unity of the two realms; that of the Reality (*al-Ḥaqq*) and that of creation (*al-khalq*), which for him, as we saw earlier, are one and the same. Al-Shirāzi, in a more specific way, identifies the possible essences with those universal entities or intelligible forms which constitute for the Sufis the World of Command (*'Alam al-Amr*) and for the Neoplatonic philosophers the intelligible world.

The second mode of diversification corresponds to the creation of the Universal Soul, of which all individual souls are so many manifestations. The Universal Soul is identified by al-Shirāzi with the Preserved Tablet, or the original codex on which the Qur'an was inscribed, and which embodies for al-Shirāzi the Eternal Decree of God and the concrete expression of His will in time, as well as His means of contact with the lower world.

As was mentioned in an earlier chapter, the soul is described in Ishraqi literature as a mixture of light and darkness, serving thereby as a link between the intelligible and material realms. The latter realm consists of the universal sphere, which embraces all the subordinate spheres as Neoplatonic cosmology, ranging in descending order from the sphere of the fixed stars or the Empyrean, through the lower worlds of generation and corruption. However, in a more specific way, the outermost sphere, due to its subtlety, separates the intelligible world of forms or souls from the material entities making up the lower world, as the diagram above shows.

Finally, despite this diversification or plurality, the whole world forms, for al-Shirāzi, a 'single jewel' with many layers diffusing the light of the Supreme Reality, throughout the whole universe, each according to the degree of its luminosity or subtlety. In that respect, the whole hierarchy represents, for al-Shirāzi, the varying degrees of divine self-manifestation or the series of lights that exhibit God's face.

The human soul differs from all created entities by virtue of the fact that it is a combination of light and darkness. It is for that reason the link between the intelligible world, or the 'world of Command', as the Sufis call it, and the material world, or the 'world of creation'. The latter begins with the universal sphere, which separates the 'world of intelligibles' or souls from the world of material or sensible entities. The diagram above illustrates the hierarchy or 'great chain of being' as presented by al-Shirāzi, with its corresponding Neoplatonic parallels. From this diagram, we can see how al-Shirāzi, like other Ishrāqi philosophers, continues the Avicennian, Neoplatonic tradition, with essential verbal or semantic variations. First, the light-radiation terminology that has given this philosophy its name is the counterpart of the intellect-intelligible terminology of the Neoplatonists; but the cosmology, as well as the metaphysical framework, is essentially the same. Al-Shirāzi, nonetheless, disagrees with Ibn Sīna on two fundamental points: the eternity of the world and the resurrection of the body. He contends that all the ancient philosophers or sages, from Hermes to Thales, Pythagoras and Aristotle, have represented the world as created in time (*muḥdath*) but it was their followers who mistakenly attributed to them the contrary view of eternity. According to al-Shirāzi, it is impossible to prove the eternity of time and motion upon which those philosophers (he probably meant the Muslim Neoplatonists) base their thesis that the world is eternal. The only being whose existence precedes that of time and motion is God, who brings the world into being by ordering it to be, as

Qur'an 3, 42 and 16, 42 put it. Now, since time is part of the universe, it is impossible that it should precede God's creative order or Command (*Amr*) which causes the world to come into being at once. The sensible and the intelligible worlds are both subject to continuous change or transformation, and accordingly cannot be eternal. Even the 'fixed entities', or intelligible forms, are susceptible of change; and although they existed originally in the divine mind, they did not have in that condition any reality or independent existence. Having come into being as a result of the divine Command, material entities can only be described as temporal or created in time. The world itself, then, must be said to be temporal or created in time (*ḥādith* or *muḥdath*).[8]

As for the second point on which he diverges from Ibn Sīna, al-Shirāzi is categorical that a person's first or 'natural birth', as he calls it, will be followed by a second birth on the Day of Resurrection. The mode of this second birth is not clearly defined, but al-Shirāzi is emphatic that on that day, humans will enter upon a higher estate in which soul and body become identical. For 'everything in the Hereafter is alive and its life is identical with its essence'.[9] More explicitly, in the Hereafter bodies and their forms are identical with their corresponding souls and the habits or traits which they had acquired in the lower world; so that the forms that people will take upon their resurrection will duplicate the habits or traits of character they had acquired while on earth. In any case, the union of soul and body, or rather their identity, is safeguarded in the Hereafter and the resurrection of the individual, regarding which al-Fārābi, Ibn Sīna and Ibn Rushd had vacillated, is unequivocally reaffirmed.

This sophisticated view, which al-Shirāzi supports with extensive quotations from the Qur'an, Hadith and sayings of the Shī'ite Imams, has the merit of safeguarding resurrection, with this subtle refinement that the resuscitated body assumes now an ethereal form and in that condition is explicitly stated to be identical with the soul.

10
Modern and contemporary trends

Islamic thought in India–Pakistan and South-East Asia

Islamic philosophy was introduced to India by the Ismā'ili propagandists (*dā'is*) as early as the late ninth century. Supported by the Fatimid rulers of Egypt, they even succeeded in founding an Ismā'ili state in Sind in 977. With the conquest of India by the founder of the Ghaznawid dynasty, Sultan Maḥmūd, the picture changed somewhat, for he put an end to Ismā'ili rule in Sind and established Lahore as his capital. Unlike Maḥmūd, his son Mas'ūd (1031–41) encouraged the study of Islamic philosophy and imported books and ideas from Khurasan in Persia. The only noteworthy scholar during the Ghaznawid period was Abū'l-Ḥasan al-Hujwiri (d. 1072), author of a mystical and metaphysical work entitled *Kashf al-Maḥjūb* (Uncovering the Hidden).

The Ghaznawid dynasty was defeated by the Ghurids, zealous patrons of learning whose reign was adorned by such distinguished scholars and philosophers as 'Aḍud al-Dīn al-Ījì (d. 1355), and Fakhr al-Dīn al-Rāzi, discussed in chapter 8.

During the Mongol period, a number of eminent scholars and theologians arose, including Ṣadr al-Dīn al-Taftāzani (d. 1390), author of a commentary on the *Creed* of al-Nasafi (d. 1142); al-Sharīf al-Jurjāni, author of *al-Ta'rifat* and a commentary on al-Ījì's *Mawāqif*; Jalāl al-Dīn al-Dawwāni (d. 1501), author of *Makārim al-Akhlāq*; Shaykh Aḥmad Sirhindi (d. 1624); and 'Abd al-Ḥakīm Sialkūti (d. 1657).

The greatest scholar of eighteenth-century India was probably Qutb al-Dīn Aḥmad, better known as Shāh Waliullah (d. 1762), who wrote a number of works on philosophical and theological subjects in both Arabic and Persian. *Shifā' al-Qulūb* (Healing the Hearts) and *al-Tafhimāt al-Ilāhiyah* (Divine Explanations) are particularly noteworthy. In the field of Sufism, Waliullah attempted to reconcile Ibn 'Arabi's *waḥdat al-wujūd*, or unity of being, and Sirhindi's *waḥdat al-shuhūd*, or unity of presence. He also tried to reconcile the four schools of Islamic law, as well as to bring together the Sunni and Shī'ite branches of Islam.[1]

As Islam came into contact with Western civilization in the nineteenth century, a 'modernist' movement began to take shape. Its best representative is Sayyid Aḥmad Khān of Bahador (d. 1898), who was born in Delhi, received a conservative education and was particularly impressed by the similarity between Christianity and Islam. According to him, this similarity was due to the fact that they were both grounded in a 'natural' morality from which the supernatural component could be expunged. This was the core of al-Afghāni's attack on the Necheriah of India in his famous *Refutation of the Materialists* or Necheris. After a short visit to England in 1870, Aḥmad Khān's enthusiasm for Western civilization heightened. On his return to India he started publication of an Urdu magazine entitled *Tahzibu-l-Akhlāq* (Cultivation of Morals), and an Urdu commentary on the Qur'an written in entirely 'naturalistic' terms. In 1875 he founded the Muḥammadan Anglo-Oriental College of Aligarh.[2]

Aḥmad Khān's most noteworthy successor in India was Sayyid Amīr 'Ali (d. 1928), who was in sympathy with the liberalism of his predecessor, but went further than him in his veneration of Prophet Muḥammad, whom he set up as the paragon of moral and spiritual excellence. For Amīr 'Ali, the spirit of Islam (the title of his best-known book) was reducible to those ideas or norms that form the core of liberalism and rationalism. Like many other apologists for Islam, Amīr 'Ali argues that Western Christianity and Western science have a solid basis in Islamic learning and that, despite the vicissitudes of time and fortune, Islam remains 'a religion of right-doing, right-thinking and right-speaking, founded on divine love, universal charity and the equality of man in the sight of the Lord'.[3] According to Amīr 'Ali, Islam is, in fact, in accord with progressive tendencies and a dynamic agent of civilization.

It should be noted, however, that despite his historical learning, Amīr 'Ali's portrayal of Islam remains essentially romantic. The most serious Indian–Pakistani interpretation of Islam in modern philosophical terms is that of Muḥammad Iqbāl (d. 1938), whose impact on Islamic thought in Pakistan has been considerable. What captured Iqbāl's imagination about European life was, on the positive side, the dynamism and vitality of this life and, on the negative side, the dehumanizing influence of capitalism on the human soul, as Wilfred C. Smith has put it.[4] The last observation strengthened his faith in the superiority of Islam as a moral and spiritual ideal, and thus he proceeded to defend this ideal in his best-known book, *Reconstruction of Religious Thought in Islam*. For Iqbāl, religion is not in opposition to philosophy, as al-Ghazāli, Ibn Taymiyah and others contended, but is rather the core of that total experience upon which philosophy must reflect, and this is borne out by the Qur'an's emphasis on knowledge and reflection. Iqbāl is critical, however, of the excessive reliance on reason exhibited by Ibn Rushd and the Mu'tazilah, on the one hand, and the anti-rationalism or scepticism of al-Ghazāli, on the other.

For Iqbāl, the Qur'anic worldview is that of a created reality in which the actual and the ideal coalesce and which exhibits a distinct rational pattern. However, the universe, according to this worldview, is not a 'block universe' or a finished product, but is rather a universe which continually realizes itself across the vast expanses of space and time, and in which humankind is the principal co-worker with God.[5] According to Iqbāl, Muslim thought's reaction against Greek philosophy was prompted by the desire to reassert the concreteness of reality, both in its empirical and its spiritual aspects. This gave rise in time to the 'inductive method', making the rise of modern European science itself possible, for it was Roger Bacon who introduced the inductive method to the West, after being introduced to it by the Arab-Muslim philosophers.[6] Nevertheless, Iqbāl is highly sympathetic to certain metaphysical aspects of modern European thought, such as Bergson's 'vital impetus', Hegel's Absolute Ego and Whitehead's process philosophy, which are far from being inductive or empirical, and which he exploits in his interpretation of the nature of reality, embedded in the Qur'an, according to him.

Regardless of whether one agrees with this interpretation or not, it is significant that Iqbāl remains one of the few modern Muslim philosophers to have been willing to apply Western philosophical categories to the interpretation of the Qur'an. Despite the vast range of his learning, Iqbāl's thought remains somewhat eclectic and his overall interpretation of the Qur'anic worldview is not always compatible with the traditional interpretations of the classical commentators.

When we turn to South-East Asia, which came under the influence of Islam as early as the thirteenth century, we are struck by the large number of writings on jurisprudence, theology and Sufism that appeared in Malay during the sixteenth and seventeenth centuries. Of these writings, the works of Ḥamzah Fansūri (d. *c.*1600) and Nūr al-Dīn al-Ranīri (d. 1666), Shams al-Dīn al-Sumaṭrāni (d. 1630) and 'Abd al-Ra'ūf al-Singkeli (d. 1693) are particularly noteworthy.[7] These writings reflect the profound impact of Sufism on Malay thinkers, who tended, on the whole, to be less discursive or philosophical than Persian or Indian scholars. However, in so far as certain forms of Sufism, such as Ibn 'Arabi's, embodied an important philosophical component, the Wujūdiyah school championed by Ḥamzah Fansūri and Shams al-Dīn Sumaṭrāni gained considerable ground in Malaysia and Indonesia, but was opposed by the more orthodox ulema, of whom the most influential was Nūr al-Dīn al-Ranīri, who accused his opponents of heresy.

During the eighteenth and nineteenth centuries, as interest in Sufism declined, so did literary output which had pitted the pro-Wujūdiyah and the anti-Wujūdiyah protagonists against each other. This situation has changed somewhat in the twentieth century, as the philosophical output of contemporary Malay scholars shows. The best-known such scholar is Muḥammad Naguib al-'Aṭṭās, who has written extensively on philosophical and Sufi subjects. Of his writings, mention might be made of the *Mysticism of Ḥamzah Fansūri*, the *Meaning and Experience of Happiness in Islam* and *Islam, Secularism and the Philosophy of the Future*.

In the last-mentioned book, al-'Aṭṭās speaks of the 'grave crisis' of contemporary Christianity, which he identifies with the modern secularization of life in the West. He then proceeds to argue that Islam has not been exposed to such a crisis. Even early Christianity was free from such exposure and accordingly it was closer to Islam to a remarkable degree, unlike contemporary Western Christianity which is in the throes of secular aberration. In Islam, contrariwise, 'we do not, unlike Christianity,' he writes, 'lean heavily, for theological and metaphysical support, on the theories of the secular philosophers, metaphysicians and scientists',[8] but rely instead on religious experience and the Revealed Law. This course is not open to Christianity, anyway, because, according to al-'Aṭṭās, it is not a revealed religion. Its basic articles of faith are, he argues, so many parts of a 'sophisticated form of culture religion', which is not even a universal religion, a characteristic that al-'Aṭṭās appears to confine exclusively to Islam.[9]

Like other fundamentalists, al-'Aṭṭās dwells on the undoubted superiority of Islam, as the only religion which is truly global and encompasses every aspect of human life, private or public, spiritual or temporal, in contradistinction to Christianity, which stresses the spiritual aspect only. In support of his claims, al-'Aṭṭās ranges over a vast number of problems and movements, from Protestantism to Catholicism, Judaism and Hinduism, and invokes the authority of innumerable philosophers and theologians, such as Parmenides, Nietzsche, Max Weber, Descartes, Von Harnack, Boethius and Aquinas, who have very often no more than a tenuous relation to the questions at issue. He often makes unwarranted statements or proposes theories which cannot possibly be corroborated. For instance, 'Religion in the sense we mean', he writes, 'has never taken root in Western civilization due to its excessive and misguided love of the world and secular life.'[10] In his discussion of the concept of religion, he resorts to arbitrary etymologies and reduces the concept of *dīn* to that of being in debt to God and even refers to an archaic usage of *dīn* as 'recurrent rain'. The other connotations of the root-verb *dāna*, such as 'to submit' or its antonym, 'to dominate', cannot be excluded, but the primary connotation of *dāna* and its derivatives in a religious context is unquestionably 'to judge' and 'judgement' respectively. It is for this reason, no doubt, that the Day of Judgement is referred to in the Qur'an (1, 3; 26, 82; 37, 20; 38, 79, etc.) as *Yawm al-Dīn*. Apart from this, the aim of al-'Aṭṭās in most of his 'philosophical' writings is distinctly polemical, and does not for that reason inform or enlighten his reader, whether Muslim or Christian.

The continuity of the Ishrāqi tradition in Persia

As we have seen, the Ishrāqi tradition reached its zenith in the impressive synthesis of Ṣadr al-Dīn al-Shirāzi during the Safawid period. Al-Shirāzi's disciples and successors included his two sons Ibrāhīm and Aḥmad, Fayāz al-Lahiji (d. 1662) and Muḥsin Fayd Kashāni (d. 1680), Muḥammad Bāqir Majlisi (d. 1700) and Ni'matullah Shustari (d. 1691). Other successors included Muḥammad Mahdi Burjurdi (d. 743) and Aḥmad al-Aḥsā'ī (d. 1828), but his most important successor was probably Mulla Hadi Sabzawāri (d. 1878), who commented on al-Shirazi's writings.

With the death of Sabzawāri, philosophical activity which had centred round the School of Isfahān moved to Tehran, producing such eminent philosophers and scholars as Mulla 'Abd Allah Zanūzi and Mulla 'Ali Zanūzi, Mirza Abū'l-Ḥasan Jilwah, Mirza Mahdi Ashtiyāni and Mirza Ṭāhir Tunikabūni. Those scholars commented on the works of al-Shirāzi and continued the tradition of the School of Isfahān of which he was the principal figure, but others, like Jilwah, accused al-Shirāzi of following the Peripatetic line, as represented by Ibn Sīna.[11]

In more recent years, the Ishrāqi tradition, with its Peripatetic and Sufi leanings, has continued to flourish in Iran. Noteworthy among its exponents during the last fifty years are Muḥammad Qāzim 'Aṣṣar, Sayyid Abū'l-Ḥasan Qazwīni and Muḥammad Ḥusayn Ṭabaṭabā'i. All those scholars commented on the works of al-Shirāzi, especially *al-Asfār al-Arba'ah*, those of Ibn Sīna, Ibn 'Arabi and other classical philosophers of Islam. The tendency of those philosophers or scholars has been to identify themselves with the Ishrāqi tradition as represented by al-Shirāzi, but it is significant that some of them, like Muḥammad Ṣālih Ḥāi'ri Māzandarāni and Ziā' al-Dīn Durri, have argued, quite rightly we believe, that al-Shirāzi was far more dependent on the Peripatetic philosophy of Ibn Sīna than his disciples and commentators have been willing to admit.

Other contemporary Iranian philosophers who have commented on the works of Ibn Sīna and al-Shirāzi include Maḥmūd Shahābi, Muḥammad Mishkāt, the 'Persian Lady',

Yak Banū-yi Irāni and Sayyid Jalal Ashtiyāni. Murtaḍa Muṭaharri has written, in addition to traditional expositions, works intended to present Islam in modern idiom, addressed to younger people.

The best known of the contemporary Iranian philosophers who have studied or taught in the West is Seyyed Hossein Nasr, whose philosophical output in English on Islamic cosmology, mysticism and metaphysics is widely known in scholarly and academic circles. As Mehdi Aminrazavi put it recently, one of Nasr's greatest achievements 'is his engagement with modern thought as an Islamic philosopher', in the process providing an Islamic response to the challenges of the modern world.[12] Mahdi Hā'iri Yazdi, who studied in Qom and Toronto, has written extensively on Ishrāqi philosophy and, like Nasr, has attempted to provide an Islamic response to the Western analytical trend in contemporary philosophy. Finally, it may be noted that the political philosophy of Ayatullah Khomeini, embodied in his *Wilāyat al-Faqīh* (The Rule of Religious Scholars) and other writings, like *Miṣbāḥ al-Hidāyah* (The Lamp of Guidance), has a definite Ishrāqi base. Mention should also be made of Ayatullah Tāliqāni, who proposed a leftist interpretation of Islam; of Ayatullah Muntaẓiri, who wrote on political philosophy and Allāmah Shari'āti who has taken a hostile attitude towards traditional Islamic philosophy and defended radical interpretations of Islam.

Modernism and fundamentalism in the Muslim world today

The final reconciliation of philosophy and Sufism at the hands of the Ishrāqi philosophers ensured a secure foothold for philosophy in Persia and ushered in the modernist age, of which Jamāl al-Dīn al-Afghāni was the chief precursor. This famous intellectual and political activist was born in Asadabad in Afghanistan in 1839. He then moved with his family to Qazwin and thence to Tehran, where he studied with Aqāṣid Ṣādiq, the most famous Shī'ite scholar of the period. From that city, he moved to Najaf in Iraq, where he studied with another leading scholar, Murtaḍa al-Anṣāri. In 1853, he visited India where he studied Western science, then embarked on a series of travels which took him to Hijāz, Egypt, Yemen, Turkey, Russia, England and France. During his second visit to Egypt in 1871 he met Muḥammad 'Abduh, destined to become his most influential disciple. Together, they moved to Paris in 1884, where they published jointly a revolutionary journal, *al-'Urwah al-Wuthqā* (The Strongest Bond), which called for the union of all the Muslim peoples and the restoration of the caliphate. In 1892, al-Afghāni visited Istanbul for the second time and was well received by Sultan 'Abd al-Ḥamīd, who saw in this Muslim scholar a welcome supporter of his own pan-Islamic goals, but association between the scholar and the Sultan eventually came to grief. Al-Afghāni died in 1897 in Istanbul.

Al-Afghāni's theological and philosophical thought is almost completely embodied in his *al-Radd 'ala'l-Dahriyīn* (Refutation of the Materialists) which he wrote in Persian and intended to be a response to Aḥmad Khān's 'naturalism' (*necheriah*). In this book, al-Afghāni dwells on the role that religion has played in the moral and spiritual progress of humankind and how the mightiest empires were often corroded from within by materialistic and atheistic movements which repudiated any form of religious belief. France, which had risen to be a great nation following the downfall of the Roman Empire, he writes, was ruined by the atheistic ideas of the French revolutionaries, and even Napoleon could not save her. He next prophesies that the Nihilists and Socialists of his day, who are intent on the elimination of private property and the abolition of religion will, if successful, lead the whole world to extinction; 'may God save us from their evil words and deeds!'[13]

Al-Afghāni's influence was in many ways perpetuated by his disciple Muḥammad 'Abduh, who laid the foundations of Islamic modernism or reformism in the Middle East. He was born in 1849 and entered al-Azhar in 1866, staying there for four years. However, he did not approve of the outmoded methods of instruction at that venerable institution, especially its neglect of the subjects of theology and philosophy. Al-Afghāni had already inaugurated the study of these two subjects in Egypt, but al-Azhar's authorities regarded their study as a form of heresy; when Muḥammad 'Abduh himself started lecturing on these subjects at al-Azhar, he was met with the same intense opposition. His students, however, received his lectures with great enthusiasm, especially when he lectured on Ibn Khaldūn's philosophy of history and tried to apply that historian's sociological and philosophical categories to the current situation in Egypt.

Muḥammad 'Abduh's theological views are embodied in his major theological treatise, entitled *Risālat al-Tawḥid* (Epistle of Unity), which opens in the traditional manner with a discussion of God's existence, His attributes and the reality of prophethood. In the latter respect, he observes, theological discourse was not unknown in pre-Islamic times, but theologians in those days tended to support their arguments by appealing to paranatural or miraculous phenomena instead of rational proof. With the rise of Islam, that picture changed completely, and reason was set up as the ultimate arbiter of moral and religious truth. 'Thus reason and religion coalesced for the first time in a sacred Book revealed to a Prophet in an explicit idiom which did not admit of any interpretation.'[14] That is why it was accepted as axiomatic in religious circles that assent to the fundamental articles of faith such as God's existence, the commissioning of prophets by God and the understanding of the intent of revelation could not be divorced from recourse to reason. Some of those articles, it is true, might appear to exceed the powers of reason, but none of them could contradict reason.

On the moral issues which split the theologians and philosophers into rival groups during the classical period, 'Abduh takes a conciliatory line. The Mu'tazilah, he argues, maintained that God, by virtue of His justice, is bound to take account of the welfare of His servants, whereas their Ash'arite and Ḥanbalite rivals rejected this thesis on the ground that God was not subject to any kind of compulsion, moral or other. The fault of the first group, according to him, is that they represent God as a servant enforcing the dictates of his master; whereas the second group represent Him as a despot who acts as He pleases. Both groups, however, agree that God's actions exhibit His wisdom and that caprice or folly cannot be attributed to Him. Therefore, believes 'Abduh, the differences between the two groups are really verbal.

On the key question of free will, 'Abduh is much more inclined to endorse the Mu'tazilite position, despite the evasive language he uses in his conciliatory effort. Reason stipulates, according to him, that rational beings who are conscious of their actions must be free, and whenever they are thwarted in carrying out their designs, they are forced to recognize that there is a higher Power in the world, which governs it and regulates every occurrence in it. To deny that human agents are free, and therefore responsible for their actions, is to deny the whole concept of religious obligation (*taklīf*) upon which the entire fabric of religious belief and practice actually rests. However, he hastens to add, in his guarded agnostic manner, that a full understanding of the relation between an individual's undoubted freedom and God's universal providence is one of those 'secrets of the divine Decree (*qadar*)' which a well-known Prophetic Tradition admonishes us not to delve into.[15]

'Abduh's moderate rationalism does not exclude assent to the messages revealed to the prophets, as we have seen. The primary function of prophethood or revelation, according to him, is the refinement of character or the confirmation of the precepts or stipulations of reason; thus, it is a mistake to seek in the Qur'an, as some modern apologists for Islam have tried to do, answers to historical or scientific questions. The purpose of astronomical, geographic or historical references in the Qur'an is simply to demonstrate the power or majesty of God, or to convey a specific moral message. In the light of these explanations, Islam, for 'Abduh, must be recognized as the most perfect or definitive revelation, communicated to Muḥammad, the last of the prophets, or their 'seal'. Better than any other revelation, this revelation has recognized humankind's dual character as citizens of this world and the next, and their duty to submit to God's ordinances and accept only those truths that reason can corroborate or confirm. Thus, Islam has liberated humanity from the shackles of all authority except that of God, and has permitted its followers to enjoy the pleasures of this life in moderation. As an instance of its all-embracing, global character, 'Abduh mentions the fact that Islam has legislated for every aspect of human life, moral, intellectual, social and spiritual. This, he claims, is an added mark of its superiority to other religions, which, like Christianity, have confined themselves to spiritual matters only.[16]

Muḥammad 'Abduh's best-known disciple was Muḥammad Rashīd Riḍa (d. 1935) who continued his master's religious message and reaffirmed al-Afghāni's call to reform and modernize Islam and unite the Muslim peoples under the banner of the Caliph. At the literary and theological levels, his activity was centred on *al-Manār* (The Lighthouse), a magazine he founded in 1898, and which he devoted to preaching the timeless message of Islam and its suitability to every age and clime. Like *al-'Urwah al-Wuthqā*, which was in a sense its predecessor, *al-Manār* was committed to the pan-Islamic ideal and the restoration of the caliphate. A pivotal message of this magazine was the duty of all Muslims to return to the ways of the 'pious ancestors', or *al-salaf al-ṣālih*, from which the Salafiyah movement, founded in 1883 by 'Abduh and al-Afghāni, derived its name. This movement, which had a large following, paved the way for the rise, in the mid-twentieth century, of the 'fundamentalist' movements which continue to rack the Muslim world today.

However, during the second half of the twentieth century, fundamentalism has gone a step beyond the Salafiyah movement in the direction of defending Islam against its detractors or critics, and has gained momentum at both the intellectual and practical levels. A chief target of its recent polemic has been the West. Thus Sayyid Qutb (d. 1966), one of fundamentalism's most influential ideological exponents, argued in his *al Islām wa Mushkilāt al-Ḥaḍārah* (Islam and the Problems of Civilization) that Western civilization had failed dismally in its attempt to solve the problems of the modern world, because of its commitment to the vacuous spiritual ideal preached by Christianity. In so far as this ideal creates a chasm between people's spiritual and temporal lives, it exposes them to a kind of schizophrenia from which only Islam can save them. For Islam, by virtue of its global character, refuses to accept the artificial dichotomy of temporal and spiritual; even the alleged conflict between science and religion is unknown to Islam. In fact, Islam has always been at one with science and has actually been instrumental in preparing the ground for the rise of modern science during the later Middle Ages. However, Qutb is explicit that the evils of science and technology which have marred modern civilization in the West should not be laid at the doorstep of Islam.[17]

In his less polemical works, such as *Ma'alim fi'l-Ṭarīq* (Milestones on the Way), Qutb argues that the aim of Islam is to liberate humankind from ignorance and religious unbelief; but since philosophical or theological discourse alone is not enough, Islam calls for *Jihād*, or holy warfare, which aims at removing all the obstacles in the way of the onward march of Islam. For only through *Jihād* can people be liberated from the 'worship' of other people who are no more than 'servants' of God, and thus be made to worship or submit to God's authority alone.[18]

Other Muslim apologists who have adopted the same anti-Western line include Muḥammad al-Bahi, who launched a vehement attack on the West in a book entitled *Recent Islamic Thought and its Relation to Western Imperialism* (1957). As the title of this book indicates, the West is accused of imperialism, not only at the political level, but at the intellectual level as well. Even eminent Muslim intellectuals or philosophers such as Ṭāha Ḥusayn and Muḥammad Iqbāl are accused of slavish subservience to the West, because they have attempted to interpret Islam in Western terms. Others, like 'Ali 'Abd al-Rāziq and Khālid Muḥammad Khālid, have distorted Islam, according to al-Bahi, and advocated the separation of the spiritual and the temporal, which is entirely alien to the spirit of Islam.

Abū'l-A'lā Mawdūdi (d. 1979), another leading fundamentalist, reaffirmed essentially the same thesis as Sayyid Qutb. The chief aim of the Islamic Movement, whose first president he became when it was founded in 1941, was to reform or remove the corrupt leadership of the Muslim peoples, as he put it, and to lead them back to God. This double aim could not be achieved, according to him, without recourse to *Jihād*, which he defines as 'the attempt to establish the divine order', by wresting leadership from the corrupt and unbelieving men who are in power. Islam demands that its followers should submit entirely to God alone and should shun every form of materialism or polytheism; it thus 'purifies the soul from self-seeking, egotism, tyranny, wantonness ... It induces feelings of moral responsibility and fosters the capacity for self-control.'[19]

Like both al-Bahi and Qutb, Mawdūdi is scathing in his critique of Western civilization, which is afflicted by three evils, according to him: secularism, nationalism and democracy. The trouble with secularism, Mawdūdi argues, is that it amounts to the exclusion of religion from all walks of life and, as Christianity teaches, pronounces religion to be an exclusively private or personal relation with God. Nationalism, which arose originally as a revolt against feudalism, states Mawdūdi, has evolved in modern times into the cult of the nation as an alternative to the cult of God. Finally, democracy, which was intended originally to liberate the masses from the yoke of their feudal oppressors, has, in our time, degenerated into the tyranny of the majority, as distinct from the community at large. In this way, it has come to sanction the opinions and wishes of the majority, even when they can be shown to be evil or unjust.

All the foregoing ideologies, according to Mawdūdi, flout the most fundamental Islamic principle, that of the exclusive worship of, or submission to, God alone. Hence, to the extent that Muslims are willing to espouse Western nationalism, democracy or secularism, they will, in fact, be abandoning their religion, betraying the Prophet and rebelling against God Himself.[20]

At the practical political level, fundamentalist ideology was implemented by the Egyptian religious movement known as the Muslim Brotherhood. In 1928 its founder, Ḥasan al-Bannā, had come under the influence of Rashīd Rīḍa, whose ideas were at the basis of the Brotherhood's political programme. In 1948, the Brotherhood was dissolved by the Egyptian authorities as a threat to the stability of the political order, and its founder was killed in the same year. Its activity throughout Egypt and other parts of the Arab world, such as Syria and Jordan, has continued in both a clandestine and an open manner, and is often hailed with enthusiasm at the popular level.

The chief challenge to fundamentalism came from a number of Muslim secularists, who repudiated the concept of theocracy, upon which the medieval institution of the Caliphate actually rested, and called for the separation of religion from politics. In that respect they were either inspired by Christian theology and

Western European thought, or sensed instinctively that political and social progress in the twentieth century was not possible without this separation. Some, such as the Azharite theologian 'Ali 'Abd al-Rāziq, have gone as far as arguing, in a classic political treatise, *al-Islām wa Uṣūl al-Ḥukm* (Islam and the Principles of Government) (1925), that Islam is an essentially religious or spiritual call to the whole of mankind and as such has no intrinsic political or national dimension. The Qur'an, the *Hadith* and the *Ijma'*, or consensus of the Muslim community, all concur in affirming the exclusively spiritual character of the Prophet's call to mankind, and accordingly the separation of politics and religion. During the early decades of Islam, it is true, argues 'Abd al-Rāziq, the Prophet was compelled under the pressure of circumstances to act as the political leader of the nascent Muslim community in Medinah, not in his capacity as prophet or religious teacher, but rather as the acknowledged head of that community. He was compelled by the force of circumstances to attend to certain legislative, judiciary and military matters, peripheral to his essential prophetic office. 'Abd al-Rāziq quotes a series of prophetic traditions (*hadiths*) in support of the thesis that the Prophet regarded political and practical matters as the business of the people themselves, who should not be swayed by political or imperial ambition, as he is reported to have told the second Caliph, 'Umar.

A quarter of a century later, a fellow Azharite, Khālid Muhammad Khālid, pursued this secularist line in somewhat more radical terms. In a book entitled *Min Hunā Nabda'* (This is Our Starting Point) (1950), he draws a sharp line of demarcation between the truly spiritual in Islam, which is universal and timeless, and the temporal, which is susceptible to constant change or development. He even injects into the argument a humanistic element, according to which Socrates, Muhammad and Christ are comrades who have preached the maxim that man is 'the sun around which the planets revolve', a maxim in which all the prophets, philosophers and moral teachers of mankind share. More recently Khālid retracted some of his bold secularist and humanist positions which, like 'Abd al-Rāziq, exposed him to the wrath of al-Azhar and the masses at large, in Egypt and elsewhere. Other secularists, like Zaki Najīb Maḥmūd, aligned themselves with logical positivism, while others still, like Abdullah Laroui and Sādiq al-'Azm, have aligned themselves with Marxism. Many others, such as Hasan Sa'b and Hisham Sharabi, have taken a liberal, pro-Western line, but those intellectuals continue to be outnumbered by the vast number of traditionalists and fundamentalists, who are intent on proclaiming the superior 'global' character of Islam, which, unlike Christianity, has legislated for both the private and public spheres of human activity, subordinating Caesar to God, rather than 'giving Caesar what is Caesar's and God what is God's', as the Gospels have put it.

Fundamentalism has achieved a certain notoriety by reason of its anti-Westernism and its open espousal of violence, sometimes identified with *jihad*, as a legitimate means of overturning foreign or non-Islamic regimes in which, as both Sayyid Qutb and Abū'l-A'lā Mawdūdi have put it, the fundamental Islamic principle of God's exclusive governance (*Hakimiyah*) is flouted. However, some moderate fundamentalists, such as Pakistani scholar and activist, Khurshid Ahmed, have called for return to the roots of Islam, embodied in the Qur'an and the *Hadith*, dispensing thereby with a fossilized corpus of law, defended by the Ulema, a rigid class of legal scholars, opposed to any form of change or innovation. Khurshid Ahmed has also called for the duty of Muslims to take note of the positive developments, 'which have taken place in the modern Western world', in the fields of science and technology; since such developments, as he has put it, 'have become part of the permanent legacy of mankind'. Muslims should approach these developments with an open mind, while remaining true to their own values. In the face of the dangers threatening Islam today, 'Muslims must be in a position to preserve and protect the moral, ethical and intellectual fiber of Islam.'

In a more specific way, the form that Islamic philosophy has taken in recent years has been either identified with jurisprudence (*fiqh*) or dialectical theology (*Kalām*), as has been the case of Mustafa 'Abd al-Rāziq (d. 1947) and his school, or the reinterpretation of Islamic philosophical and theological concepts in modern Western terms. At the centre of the latter pro-Western trend has been the urge to re-evaluate the Muslim heritage (*Turath*) and defend it by such contemporary intellectuals and philosophers as Muhammad 'Ābid al-Jābiri, Abdullah Laroui and Zaki Najīb Maḥmūd. In addition, the second half of the twentieth century has witnessed a widespread espousal of such Western ideologies as positivism, socialism existentialism and Marxism.

Positivism was first advocated in the Arab world by a Lebanese philosopher and doctor, Shibli Shumayyil (d. 1917). He was one of the earliest champions of Darwinian evolution, and in the manner of Herbert Spencer and Ludwig Büchner, Sumayyil applied this to the diagnosis of the Arab cultural and social ills at the turn of the century. The chief champion of positivism in more recent years has been the already-mentioned Zaki Najīb Maḥmūd, who in a number of works, including *Nahwa Falsafah 'Ilmiyah* (Towards a Scientific Philosophy) (1959) and *Tajdid al-Fikr al-'Arabi* (Renewal of Arab Thought) (1971), has argued that the chief ills afflicting Arabic thought have been verbalism, or the cult of language, on the one hand, and traditionalism, or the unquestioning adherence to outworn ideas or values, on the other, and that these have been the major bars to progress. 'I do not doubt for a single moment', he writes in the *Renewal of Arabic Thought*, 'that this road, the road of progression from backwardness to modernity lies in the transition from a mode of knowledge based on words to one whose principal component is the productive machine.' For this reason, the Arabs should give up the useless 'word industry', which has plagued Arab culture throughout the ages and in which words became surrogates for things or actions and replace it by a productive industry based on science and technology.

Friedrich Engels has made a distinction in *Historical Materialism* (1892) between two types of socialism, the Franco-British or utopian, and the 'scientific' or Marxist type, which is not merely a programme of social and economic reform, but a global philosophy superseding all other philosophies. Thus, some intellectuals, such as Qāsim Amin (d. 1908) and Salāmah Musa (d. 1959), have advocated the first variety of socialism as a means of bringing about social and political change through peaceful or constitutional reform inspired by European models. Arab Marxists, on the other hand, have favoured revolutionary action and probed the Arab-Islamic heritage for dialectical-materialist elements, as Tayyib Tizayni, Husain Muruwwa and others have done. They have gone as far as labelling the philosophy of Averroes, the great Arab-Aristotelian, as materialistic, on the ground that it represented the antithesis of Platonic idealism. Other Marxists, such as Sādiq al-'Azm have targeted the supernaturalism of Islam in a revolutionary treatise, the *Critique of Religious Thought* (1969), while others, such as Laroui, have been preoccupied with 'the crisis of the Arab intellectual', which is the title of his best-known book, written originally in French. According to Laroui, the 'tragedy' of the Arab intellectual is that he belongs to a community that has been reduced to political and intellectual subjection to European imperialism and modes of thought. As a result, the Arab intellectual has been alienated from his own culture and stripped of his national identity under the pressure of Western liberalism. Only Marxism promises to liberate him from this alienation and reconcile him to his own tradition. For only in dialectical materialism, which is the essence of Marxism, is the reconciliation of subjective truth and popular or national allegiance possible, by means of the Marxist *praxis*. In addition, due to its internationalism, Laroui appears to think, Marxism can serve as the antidote to both European nationalism and its by-product, European Imperialism.

The third major brand of Western thought to have had a significant impact on contemporary Arabic thought is existentialism. Its best-known exponents in recent years have been Rene Habachi in Lebanon, 'Abd al-Rahmān Badawi in Egypt and 'Abd al-Azīz Lahbabi in Morocco. Badawi, who is a well-known historian of Islamic philosophy, has expounded in two early works, *al-Zaman al-Wujudi* (Existential Time) (1943) and *Dirāsāt fi'l-Falsafah al-Wujūdiyah* (Studies in Existentialist Philosophy) (1961), a brand of existentialism affiliated to Martin Heidegger's concept of being-in-time (*Dasein*); whereas Habachi has expounded, both in French and Arabic, a 'personalist' or Christian existentialism affiliated to the personalism of Charles Renouvier and the Christian existentialism of Gabriel Marcel, which are diametrically opposed to the atheistic existentialism of Jean-Paul Sartre and Martin Heidegger. Lahbabi's brand of existentialism is akin to the personalist variety, but lacks its religious underpinnings.

Conclusion

Philosophy, which found its way into the Muslim world as early as the eighth century, was in constant interaction with theology and mysticism, as this study has shown. After four centuries of substantive elaboration and internal strife, the intellectual energy that had generated Islamic philosophy and theology or their offshoots was virtually spent, at least in the western parts of the Islamic world. From Muslim Spain, where it had found a final refuge, philosophy began its migration across the Pyrenees to Western Europe, and by the beginning of the thirteenth century almost all the chief monuments of Arab-Muslim philosophy, science and medicine had been translated into Latin by such eminent translators as Gerard of Cremona (d. 1187), Michael the Scot (d. 1235), Hermann the German (d. 1272) and many others. The most influential Muslim philosopher to leave a lasting imprint on Western philosophy and theology was Ibn Rushd, known in Latin as Averroes. When his commentaries on Aristotle were translated into Latin, they caused a genuine stir in philosophical and theological circles. Some theologians, known as the Latin Averroists, with Siger de Brabant (d. 1281) at their head, found in the Arab commentator a champion of what was called the Double Truth, according to which a proposition could be true in philosophy, but not true in theology, or vice versa. This gambit appeared to them to solve the perennial problem of the conflict of philosophy and theology, reason and faith. Others, with St Thomas Aquinas (d. 1274) at their head, rejected a number of Averroes' propositions on a variety of grounds. It is certain, however, that the Latin translations of Ibn

Rushd, Ibn Sīna and other Muslim philosophers were instrumental in reviving the study of Aristotelianism, which had been forgotten in the West almost from the time of Boethius (d. 525).

At the theological level, the impact of *Kalām* was far less restricted. A number of Scholastic theologians, such as Raymond Martin (d. 1286) and Raymond Lull (d. 1315), appear to have had some acquaintance with Islamic theology, but their interest, as illustrated by Raymond Martin's *Pugio Fidei*, was really polemical. The Scholastic theologian who had more than a casual knowledge of *Kalām* was St Thomas Aquinas, generally regarded as the greatest Catholic theologian of all time. Basing his work on Maimonides' summary of the major propositions of *Kalām* in his *Guide of the Perplexed*, written originally in Arabic, and known in Latin as *Dux Perplexorum*, St Thomas attempted the most thorough analysis and critique of (Ash'arite) theology to have come down to us.

The other phase of the revival of Islamic philosophy and mysticism may be termed the Persian or Ishrāqi. Inaugurated by al-Suhrawardi, as we have seen, this phase is marked by a positive move to reconcile philosophy and mysticism, in a manner which Ibn Sīna envisaged but did not implement. In addition, the Ishrāqi tradition, which culminated in the 'transcendental wisdom' of al-Shirāzi, known in Persia as Mulla Ṣadra, did not lead to the kind of embarrassment or hostility to philosophy that Ash'arite theology tended to generate, even in philosophical circles. The continuity of the Ishrāqi tradition in Iran today is attested by the large number of theological institutes in Qom, Meshhed and Tehran, as well as in Najaf, in Iraq, which continue the tradition of Ishrāqi philosophical and theological scholarship, and by the galaxy of scholars who continue to study the works of the Ishrāqi masters.

With respect to mysticism, its earliest expression, as we have seen, was asceticism, championed in the seventh and eighth centuries by al-Ḥasan al-Baṣri and his school. It grew in time into an intense spiritual movement, known as Sufism, which took two distinct forms, the 'visionary' and the 'unitary' as we might call them. The adepts of the former, like al-Junayd and al-Ghazāli, maintained that the ultimate goal of the mystic was vision (*mushāhadah, mukāshafah*); whereas the adepts of the latter, in Hindu fashion, maintained that in the final phase of the mystical experience, the mystic was united with the One or the Truth (*al-Ḥaqq*), and in this union (*ittiḥād*) the dissolution or the extinction of the self was complete.

As one would expect, this extravagant form of mysticism met with staunch opposition and was never reconciled with Sunnite orthodoxy. However, it is significant that the Ishrāqi philosophers were able to reconcile it to philosophy by adapting Ibn 'Arabi's doctrine of the 'unity of being', which had an important metaphysical and cosmological component. In that respect, the Ishrāqi tradition marks the culmination of Islamic philosophy and mysticism, and is, in fact, the only brand of Islamic philosophy to have survived up to the present time. As was mentioned earlier, it is still taught and studied in religious institutions in Iran and elsewhere.

The second encounter with Western thought in the nineteenth century generated an intellectual resurgence in the Arab-Muslim world, generally referred to as the Renaissance (*al-Nahḍah*). It was triggered in the first instance by Napoleon's expedition to Egypt in 1798, which brought the Arab-Muslim world into contact with French Revolutionary ideas, including secularism and positivism.

Two of the champions of secularism at the turn of the century were the Lebanese Farah Antun (d. 1922) and Shibli Shumayyil (d. 1917). The former based his ideas on Averroes' brand of Aristotelian rationalism; a secularist-humanist thesis which brought him into direct confrontation with the leading Egyptian theologian and scholar, Muḥammad 'Abduh (d. 1905), whose moderate 'modernism' has already been discussed. The pivotal point of the controversy was the compatibility of Islam with secularism. This, according to Muḥammad 'Abduh, tended to limit the role of God in the management of human affairs to the spiritual realm, in the manner of Christianity. In Islam, God's role in the management of these affairs is regarded as global – a thesis that has been at the centre of contemporary Islamic fundamentalism.

Shibli Shumayyil was one of the earliest Arab advocates of positivism, or the application of Western categories borrowed from French writers, such as Auguste Comte, to the solution of the Arabs' social and political problems. He also defended in French fashion, like his predecessor Rifā'ah al-Ṭahṭāwi (d. 1833), the constitutional idea, and inveighed vehemently against the despotic regimes of his day, contrasting European countries, governed by laws, with 'Eastern' countries, governed by persons who have no respect for the liberty or welfare of their subjects.

The nineteenth-century Arab Renaissance continued into the second quarter of the twentieth century. The First World War and the subsequent partitioning of the European powers, notably England and France, of the Arab countries freed from Ottoman rule in 1918, and the beginning of the colonial era in the Near East, led gradually to disenchantment with European ideologies in nationalistic circles. In the mid-twentieth century, as we have seen, many Arab intellectuals found in Marxism the ideological antidote to Western liberalism. Even those intellectuals who were not committed to Marxism welcomed it as a viable alternative to Western liberalism. No wonder that many contemporary Arab and Muslim intellectuals and political leaders have been unanimous in decrying the evils of Western imperialism. Hence a major component of Islamic fundamentalism has been anti-Westernism, couched sometimes in anti-Christian religious terms, as we have seen in the case of Sayyid Qutb and Abū'l-A'lā Mawdūdi. However, it is fair to say that the attack on

Western imperialism has not been confined to the fundamentalists, since the pro-Western secularists themselves have often seen in it a betrayal of the European ideals of liberty and equality, which, as early as the eighteenth century, were recognized by the French Revolutionaries as universal.

Appendix 1
The chief philosophical translations

The major philosophical texts translated into Arabic, either from Greek or Syriac, with the names of their known translators, are listed below.

1. Of Plato's *Dialogues*, the following were translated from Galen's synopses or epitomes:

   The Sophist, translated by Isḥāq Ibn Ḥunayn;
   Timaeus, translated by Ibn al-Biṭrīq and Yaḥia Ibn 'Adi;
   Parmenides, translated by Ḥunayn Ibn Isḥāq and 'Isa Ibn Yaḥia;
   The Crito, translated by Ḥunayn Ibn Isḥāq and 'Isa Ibn Yaḥia;
   The Laws, translated by 'Isa Ibn Yaḥia and Ibn al-Bitrīq;
   The Cratylus, translated by Ḥunayn Ibn Isḥāq and 'Isa Ibn Yaḥia;
   The Republic (*Politeia*), translated by Ḥunayn Ibn Isḥāq and 'Isa Ibn Yaḥia;
   The Phaedo, translated by Ḥunayn Ibn Isḥāq and 'Isa Ibn Yaḥia;
   Euthydemus, translated by Ḥunayn Ibn Isḥāq and 'Isa Ibn Yaḥia.

2. Of Aristotle's works, the following were translated:

   (a) Logic:
   The Categories, translated by Isḥāq Ibn Ḥunayn and others;

Hermeneutica, translated by Isḥāq Ibn Ḥunayn and others;
Analytica priora, translated by Tadhāri (Theodore) and revised by Ḥunayn Ibn Isḥāq;
Analytica posteriora, translated by Isḥāq Ibn Ḥunayn and Abū Bishr Mattā;
Sophistica, translated by Yaḥia Ibn 'Adi and 'Isa Ibn Zur'ah;
Topica, translated by Yaḥia Ibn 'Adi and Abū 'Uthmān al-Dimashqi;
Rhetorica, translated by Isḥāq Ibn Ḥunayn and Ibrāhīm al-Kātib;
Poetica, translated by Abū Bishr Mattā.

(b) The physical treatises:
The Physics, translated by Isḥāq Ibn Ḥunayn and Qusṭa Ibn Lūqa;
Generation and Corruption, translated by Isḥāq Ibn Ḥunayn and Abū 'Uthmān al-Dimashqi;
On the Heavens, translated by Yaḥia Ibn al-Biṭrīq and Abū Bishr Mattā;
Meteorologica, translated by Yaḥia Ibn 'Adi and al-Ḥasan Ibn Suwār;
The Book of Animals, translated by Yaḥia Ibn al-Biṭriq and Ibn Zur'ah;
De anima, translated by Ibn al-Biṭrīq and Isḥāq Ibn Ḥunayn;
De plantis (spurious), translated by Isḥāq Ibn Ḥunayn.

(c) *Metaphysics*:
Translated by Asṭāt, Isḥāq Ibn Ḥunayn and Yaḥia Ibn 'Adi.

(d) The ethical and political treatises:
The Nicomachean Ethics, translated by Isḥāq Ibn Ḥunayn;
The Secret of Secrets (spurious), translated by Yaḥia Ibn al-Biṭrīq;
The Politics, first translated in 1957, by Augustine Barabara.

3. Plotinus, Proclus and Porphyry:

   Athulugia or *Book of Divinity* in the *Commentary* of Porphyry, translated by 'Abd al-Masīḥ Ibn Nā'imah al-Ḥimṣi;
   The Pure Good (*Liber de causis*), translator unknown;
   Porphyry's Commentary on the Nicomachean Ethics in twelve Books, translated by Isḥāq ibn Ḥunayn;
   Isagoge of Porphyry, translated by Abū 'Uthmān al-Dimashqi.

4. Galen's philosophical and logical writings:

   Summary of Ethics, translated by Ḥunayn Ibn Isḥāq;
   Al-Burhān, translated by Ḥunayn Ibn Isḥāq;
   Introduction to Logic, translator unknown;
   The Unmoved Mover, translated by Ḥunayn Ibn Isḥāq;
   The Number of the Syllogisms, translated by Isḥāq Ibn Ḥunayn;
   That Every Virtuous Physician is also a Philosopher, translator unknown;
   Pinax, or 'Inventory of his Writings', translated by Ḥunayn Ibn Isḥāq.

5. Miscellaneous Aristotelian commentaries by Alexander of Aphrodisias, Olympiodorus, Theophrastus, Simplicius, Syrianus, Philoponus and others were in circulation, but their translators are unknown in most cases.

6. Pseudo-Plutarch:
   Placita Philosophorum, translated by Qusṭa Ibn Lūqa.

Appendix 2

Leading Mu‘tazilite scholars

The leading Mu‘tazilite scholars belonging to the two branches of Basrah and Baghdad were as follows:

The Basrah Branch:

Wāṣil Ibn ‘Atā’ (d. 748)
‘Amr Ibn ‘Ubayd (d. 760)
Yunus al-Aswāri (d. 815)
Hishām al-Fuwati (d. 833)
Mu‘ammar Ibn ‘Abbād (d. 834)
Ibrāhīm al-Naẓẓām (d. 835/845)
Abū Bakr al-Aṣamm (contemporary of al-Naẓẓām)
Abū'l-Hudhayl al-'Allāf (d. 841/849)
‘Abbad Ibn Sulaymān (d. 844)
Abū Ya‘qūb al-Shaḥḥām (d. 880)
‘Amr Ibn Baḥr al-Jāhiẓ (d. 868)
Abū ‘Ali al-Jubā'i (d. 915)
Abū Hāshim, son of al-Jubā'i (d. 933)

The Baghdad Branch:

Bishr Ibn al-Mu'tamir (d. 825)
Thumāmah Ibn Ashras (d. 828)
Abū Mūsa al-Mirdār (d. 841)
Ja‘far Ibn Mubashshir (d. 848)
Ja‘far Ibn Ḥarb (d. 851)

Aḥmad Ibn Abī Du'ād (d. 855)
Abū Ja'far al-Iskāfi (d. 855)
Abū Ḥusayn al-Khayyāt (d. 902)
Abū'l-Qāsim al-Balkhi (d. 931)
Al-Qādi 'Abd al-Jabbār (d. 1025)

Notes

Chapter 1

1. See appendix 1 for a list of major translations from Greek and Syriac.
2. Miskawayh, *Jāwidan Khirad*, pp. 5f.

Chapter 2

1. Al-Shahrastāni, *al-Milal wa'l-Niḥal*, I, p. 116.
2. Ibid.
3. Ibid., I, p. 140.
4. 'Abdullah Ibn Qutaybah, *Kitāb al-Ma'ārif* (Cairo 1969) p. 441. It is noteworthy that the Arabic term *qadar*, which means power or capacity, could be applied indifferently to humans or God, as often happened.
5. Cf. Fakhry, *al-Fikr al-Akhlāqi al-'Arabi*, p. 20.
6. Cf. Migne, *Patrologia Graeca*, XCIV, p. 1589.
7. Al-Shahrastāni, *al-Milal wa'l-Niḥal*, I, p. 78.
8. See appendix 2 for a list of leading Mu'tazilite theologians of the Basrah and Baghdad Schools.

Chapter 3

1. Al-Kindi, *Rasā'il al-Falsafiyah*, I, p. 97.
2. Ibid., p. 104.
3. Ibid., p. 105. Cf. W. D. Ross (trans.), *Select Fragments* (Oxford, 1952), Fr. 51 (*Protrepticus*).
4. Ibid., pp. 244f.
5. Al-Shahrastāni, *al-Milal wa'l-Niḥal*, I, p. 94.
6. Al-Kindi, *Rasā'il al-Falsafiyah*, I, p. 373.
7. Ibid., p. 162.

8. Ibid., p. 207.
9. Aristotle later abandoned the view that generation and corruption was a form of motion.
10. Ibid., p. 260.
11. Ibid., pp. 355f.
12. Al-Kindi, *al-Hīlah li-Daf' al-Aḥzān*, in Fakhry, *al-Fikr al-Akhlāqi al-'Arabi*, pp. 25f.
13. Al-Rāzi, *al-Ṭibb al-Rūḥāni*, in Fakhry, *al-Fikr al-Akhlāqi al-'Arabi*, p. 263.
14. Ibid.
15. Ibid., p. 286.
16. The Arabic *al-'ajam* could also denote 'foreigners' in general.
17. Al-A'sam, *Tārikh Ibn al-Riwandi*, p. 128.
18. See Khalil Samir and Nielson (eds), *Christian–Arabic Apologetics*, pp. 172f.
19. A reference to the pilgrimage to Makkah, during which Muslims are supposed to cast stones at Satan and kiss the Black Stone at the Ka'abah.
20. Edward Fitzgerald (trans.), *The Rubāiyāt of Omar Khayyām* (London, B. Quaritch, 1868), quatrains 57–8, 76, 35.

Chapter 4

1. In the Arabic tradition, two spurious works, *On Plants* and *On Minerals*, were added to the Aristotelian corpus and a supplement of the *Heavens*, called the *World*..
2. Al-Fārābi, *Iḥṣā' al-'Ulūm*, p. 99
3. Al-Fārābi, *al-Madīnah al-Fāḍilah*, p. 32. Cf. Aristotle, *Metaphysics*, XII, 1072b 18.
4. *Al-Madīnah al-Fāḍilah*, p. 39.
5. Al-Fārābi, *Risālah fi'l 'Aql*, p. 3.
6. Ibid., p. 9.
7. Cf. *al-Madīnah al-Fāḍilah*, pp. 109f.
8. Cf. *al-Shifā'* (*Ilāhiyāt*), I, pp. 60f.
9. *Al-Najāt*, p. 261. Cf. *al-Shifā'*, I, pp. 327f.

10. Cf. *al-Najāt*, pp. 271f.
11. Cf. *al-Shifā' (Ilāhiyāt)*, II, p. 356.
12. *Al-Najāt*, p. 283.
13. Ibid.
14. Ibid., p. 197. Cf. Aristotle, *De anima*, II, 412a30.
15. *Al-Najāt*, p. 328.
16. Ibid., p. 206. Cf. Ibn Sīnah, *Aḥwal al-Nafs*, pp. 114f.
17. Ibid., p. 125. The third part of the soul, according to Plato, was the rational, and his tripartite theory was almost universally accepted by Muslim philosophers and ethical writers.
18. Cf. Ṣā'id al-Andalusi, *Ṭabaqāt al-Umam*, p. 22.
19. *Al-Najāt*, Appendix A, p. 24.
20. *Rasā'il Ikhwān al-Ṣafā*, I, p. 42.
21. Ibid., I, p. 21.
22. Pythagoras was actually born on the island of Samos in the Aegean, around 572 BCE, and founded a secret religious society in Crotona in Italy.
23. *Rasā'il*, III, p. 178.
24. Ibid., p. 8.
25. Ibid., p. 137.
26. Ibid., p. 23.
27. Ibid., p. 30. Cf. Plato, *Theaetetus*, 176b.
28. *Rasā'il*, III, p. 71.

Chapter 5

1. Cf. al-Tawḥīdi, *al-Imtā' wa'l-Mu'ānasah*, II, p. 9.
2. Cf. al-Ash'ari, *Istiḥsān al-Khawḍ fī 'Ilm al-Kalām*, in McCarthy, *Theology of al-Ash'ari*, p. 95.
3. Al-Shahrastāni, *al-Milal wa'l-Niḥal*, I, p. 95.
4. Cf. al-Ash'ari, *al-Ibānah 'an Uṣūl al-Diyānah*, p. 54.
5. Ibid., pp. 7f. Cf. McCarthy, *Theology of al-Ash'ari*, pp. 238f.
6. Al-Bāqillāni, *Kitāb al-Tamhīd*, p. 18.
7. As reported by al-Baghdādi in *Uṣūl al-Dīn*, pp. 67 and 45.
8. Al-Ghazāli, *al-Munqidh min al-Ḍalāl*, p. 18.
9. Al-Ghazāli, *Tahāfut al-Falāsifah*, p. 9.

10. Ibid., p. 182.
11. Ibid., p. 364.
12. Ibid., p. 276.

Chapter 6

1. Cf. al-Qushayri, *al-Risālah al-Qushayriyah*, p. 188.
2. Badawi, *Rābi'ah*, p. 151.
3. Ibid., p. 123. Cf. M. Smith, *Studies in Early Mysticism*, p. 223.
4. Cf. Massignon, *Essai*, pp. 221f.
5. Al-Qushayri, *al-Risālah al-Qushayriyah*, p. 584.
6. Badawi, *Shaṭaḥāt al-Sūfiyah*, p. 116.
7. Zaehner, *Hindu and Muslim Mysticism*, p. 112.
8. Badawi, *Shaṭaḥāt al-Sūfiyah*, p. 116.
9. Cf. Massignon, *La Passion d'al-Hallāj*, pp. 289f and Ibn Khallikān, *Wafayāt al-A'yān*, p. 186.
10. Al-Ghazāli, *al-Munqidh*, p. 39.
11. Al-Ghazāli, *Mishkāt al-Anwār*, pp. 55–6. Cf. Qur'an 28, 88: 'Everything is perishable, save His Face.'
12. *Mishkāt al-Anwār*, p. 77.
13. *Al-Munqidh*, p. 14.
14. *Mishkāt, al-Anwār*, p. 92.
15. *Al-Munqidh*, p. 38. The thesis of extinction in unity, as well as 'extinction in extinction', is fully developed in *Iḥyā' 'Ulūm al-Dīn*, IV, p. 243.
16. *Mishkāt al-Anwār*, p. 92.
17. Cf. Fakhry, *Ethical Theories in Islam*, pp. 196f.
18. Cf. Ibn 'Arabi, *Fuṣūs al-Ḥikam*, pp. 38f and 63.
19. Cf. Affifi, *The Mystical Philosophy of Ibnu'l-'Arabi*, pp. 10f.

Chapter 7

1. Cf. Ṣā'id al-Andalusi, *Ṭabaqāt al-Umam*, p. 63.
2. Ibid., p. 83.
3. Fakhry, *Ibn Bājjah, Opera metaphysica*, p. 179.

4. Ibid., p. 62.
5. Ibid., pp. 49f.
6. Ibid., p. 172.
7. Ibid., p. 142.
8. Cf. Ibn Rushd, *Talkhīs Kitāb al-Nafs*, p. 90.
9. Ibn Ṭufayl, *Ḥayy Ibn Yaqẓān*, p. 55.
10. Ibid., p. 63.
11. Al-Shahrastāni, *al-Mila wa'l-Niḥal*, I, p. 95.
12. Ibn Rushd, *Faṣl al-Maqāl*, p. 2.
13. Ibn Rushd quotes verses 59, 2 and 7, 184, which speak of 'reflection' and 'consideration' of created things.
14. *Faṣl al-Maqāl*, p. 6.
15. *Tahāfut al-Tahāfut*, p. 180. Cf. *Tafsīr Mā Ba'd al-Ṭabī*, III, p. 1399.
16. Cf. *al-Kashf*, p. 118; *Tahāut al-Tahāfut*, p. 582.
17. Cf. *Tahāfut al-Tahāfut*, p. 522. Cf. Aristotle, *Analytica posteriora*, 1, 2 *passim*.
18. *Al-Kashf*, p. 41. Cf. *Tahāfut al-Tahāfut*, p. 520.
19. Ibn Rushd quotes in this connection Qur'an 22, 72 and 7, 184.
20. Cf. Ibn Rushd, *Hal Yattaṣil bi'l-'Aql al-Hayūlāni al-'Aql al-Fa' 'āl?* in *Talkīs Kitāb al-Nafs*, pp. 119f.

Chapter 8

1. Cf. Ibn Taymiyah, *Majmū'at al-Rasā'il*, I, p. 16.
2. Ibid., pp. 100 and 190.
3. Ibid., pp. 160f and 180f.
4. Cf. Ibn Taymiyah, *al-Radd 'alā al-Manṭiqiyīn*, pp. 124f.
5. Cf. al-Rāzi, *al-Mabāḥith*, I, pp. 25f.
6. Cf. ibid., p. 470 and *al-Muḥaṣṣal*, pp. 127f.
7. Cf. Ibn Khaldūn, *al-Muqaddimah*, p. 435.
8. Ibid., p. 516.
9. Ibid., p. 517.
10. Ibid., p. 518.
11. Ibid., p. 519.
12. Ibid., p. 143.

Chapter 9

1. Cf. al-Suhrawardi, *Ḥikmat al-Ishrāq*, pp. 10f.
2. Ibid., pp. 106f.
3. The terms conquest and love correspond to the two powers of *neikos* and *philia*, which according to Empedocles govern the world. They are often referred to in the Arabic sources.
4. Cf. al-Suhrawardi, *Ḥikmat al-Ishrāq*, p. 252.
5. Cf. al-Shirāzi, *al-Asfār*, II, pp. 246f.
6. Cf. al-Shirāzi, *Kitāb al-Mashā'ir*, pp. 13f.
7. Cf. *al-Asfār*, I, p. 14 and *Kitāb al-Mashā'ir*, p. 37.
8. Cf. al-Shirāzi, *Risālah fi'l-Ḥudūth*, in *Rasā'il Akhund*, pp. 45f.
9. Al Shirāzi, *al-Ḥashr wa'l-Nushūr*, p. 45.

Chapter 10

1. Cf. Nasr and Leaman, *History of Islamic Philosophy*, II, pp. 1068f.
2. Cf. W. C. Smith, *Modern Islam in India*, pp. 16f.
3. Amir 'Ali, *The Spirit of Islam*, p. 178.
4. Cf. W. C. Smith, *Modern Islam in India*, p. 102.
5. Cf. Iqbāl, *Reconstruction of Religious Thought in Islam*, pp. 4f.
6. Ibid., p. 123.
7. Cf. Nasr and Leaman, *History of Islamic Philosophy*, II, p. 1135.
8. Al-'Aṭṭas, *Islam, Secularism and the Philosophy of the Future*, p. 23.
9. Ibid., p. 27.
10. Ibid., p. 129.
11. Cf. Nasr and Leaman, *History of Islamic Philosophy*, II, pp. 1037f. and Browne, *Literary History of Persia*, pp. 111 and 400f.
12. Nasr and Leaman, *History of Islamic Philosophy*, II, p. 1041.
13. Al-Afghāni, *al-Radd 'alā al-Dahriyīn*, p. 62.
14. 'Abduh, *Riṣālat al-Tawḥīd*, p. 25.
15. Ibid., p. 91.
16. Ibid., p. 138.
17. Qutb, *al-Islām wa Mushkilāt al-Ḥaḍārah*, p. 168.
18. Cf. Qutb, *Ma'ālim fi'l-Ṭarīq*, p. 62.
19. Mawdūdi, *Moral Foundations*, p. 99.
20. Ibid., p. 41.

Select bibliography

Arabic sources

'Abduh, Muḥammad. *Risālat al-Tawḥīd*, Cairo, 1963
'Abd al-Jabbar, Abū'l Ḥasan. *Al-Mughni*, 15 vols, Cairo, 1961–5
'Abū Rīda, 'Abd al-Hādi (ed.). *Rasā'l al-Kindi al-Falsafiyah*, 2 vols, Cairo, 1950–3
al-Afghāni, Jamāl al-Dīn. *Al-Radd 'ala'l-Dahriyīn* (Arabic), Cairo and Baghdad, 1955
al-Andalusi, Ṣā'id Ibn Ṣā'id. *Ṭabaqāt al-Umam*, Beirut, 1912
al-Ash'ari, Abū'l-Ḥasan. *Al-Ibānah 'an Uṣūl al-Diyānah*, Hyderabad, 1948
Istiḥsān al Khawḍ fī 'Ilm al-Kalām, in *Theology of al-Ash'ari*, ed. R. J. McCarthy, Beirut, 1953
Maqalāt al-Islāmiyīn, Istanbul, 1939–40
al-A'sam, 'Abd al-Amīr. *Tārikh Ibn al-Riwandi al-Mulḥid*, Beirut, 1975
al-'Aẓm, Sādiq. *Naqd al-Fikr al-Dīni*, Beirut, 1969
Badawi, 'Abd al-Raḥmān (ed.). *Arisṭu 'ind al-'Arab*, Cairo, 1947
—— *Aflutīn 'ind al-'Arab*, Cairo, 1955
—— *Rābi'ah, Shahīdat al-'Ishq al-Ilāhi*, Cairo, n.d.
—— *Shaṭaḥāt al-Sūfiyah*, Cairo, 1949
al-Baghdādi, Abd al-Qāhir. *Al-Farq bain al-Firaq*, Cairo, 1910
—— *Uṣūl al-Dīn*, Istanbul, 1928
al-Bāqillāni, Abū Bakr. *Kitāb al-Tāmhīd*, Beirut, 1957
al-Birūni, Abū'l-Rayḥān. *Taḥqīq mā li'l-Hind min Maqūlah*, London, 1887
al-Bukhāri, Muḥammad. *Al-Jāmi' al-Ṣaḥīh*, Leyden, 1862–1908
Fakhry, Mājid (ed.). *Al-Fikr al-Akhlāqi al-'Arabi*, Beirut, 1978
—— *Ibn Bājjah, Opera metaphysica*, Beirut, 1968
al-Fārābi, Abū Naṣr. *Fuṣūl Muntaza'ah*, Beirut, 1971

—— *Iḥṣā' al-'Ulum*, Cairo, 1949
—— *Al-Jam' bayna Ra'yay al-Ḥakimayn*, Beirut, 1960
—— *Kitāb al-Ḥuruf*, Beirut, 1970
—— *Mabādi Ārā' Ahl al-Madīnah al-Fāḍilah*, Beirut, 1959
—— *Risālah fi'l-'Aql*, Beirut, 1960
—— *Taḥsil al-Sa'ādah*, Beirut, 1981
al-Ghazāli, Abū Ḥāmid. *Iḥyā' 'Ulūm al-Dīn*, Cairo, 1929
—— *Al-Iqtiṣād fi'l-I'tiqād*, Cairo, n.d.
—— *Maqāsid al-Falāsifah*, Cairo, 1913
—— *Mishkāt al-Anwār*, Cairo, 1964
—— *Al-Munqidh min al-Ḍalāl*, Beirut, 1959
—— *Tahāfut al-Falāsifah*, Beirut, 1927
Ibn Abī Uṣaybi'ah, Ahmad. *'Uyūn al-Anbā'*, Beirut, 1965
Ibn Bājjah, Abū Bakr. *Opera metaphysica*, ed. M. Fakhry, Beirut, 1968
Ibn Fātik, al-Mubashshir. *Mukhtār al-Ḥikam*, Madrid, 1958
Ibn 'Arabi, Muḥyid-Dīn. *Fuṣūs al-Ḥikam*, Cairo, 1949
—— *Al-Futuḥāt al-Makkiyah*, Cairo, n.d.
Ibn Ḥazm, 'Ali ibn Aḥmad. *Al-Akhlāq wa'l-Siyar*, Beirut, 1961
—— *Al-Fiṣal fi'l-Milal wa'l-Ahwā' wa'l-Niḥal*, Cairo, 1899
Ibn Khaldūn, Abd al-Raḥmān. *Al-Muqaddimah*, Cairo, n.d.
—— *Al-Ta'rif bi'Ibn Khaldūn*, Cairo, 1951
Ibn Khallikān. *Wafayāt al-A'yān*, Cairo, 1949
Ibn al-Nadīm, Muḥammad. *Kitāb al-Fihrist*, Cairo, n.d.
Ibn Rushd, Abū'l Walīd. *Tafsīr mā Ba'd al-Tabi'ah*, 5 vols, Beirut, 1938–55
—— *Faṣl al-Maqāl* and *al-kashf 'an Manāhij al-Adillah*, in *Falsafat Ibn Rushd*, Cairo, 1901
—— *Tahāfut al-Tahāfut*, Beirut, 1930
—— *Talkhīs Kitāb al-Nafs*, Cairo, 1950
Ibn Sīna, Abū 'Ali al-Ḥusayn. *Aḥwāl al-Nafs*, Cairo, 1952
—— *Al-Ishārāt wa'l-Tanbihāt*, Cairo, 1957–60
—— *Mantiq al-Mashriqiyīn*, Cairo, 1910
—— *Al-Najāt*, Beirut, 1986
—— *Al-Shifā'(Ilāhiyāt)*, Cairo, 1960
Ibn Taymiyah, Taqiy al-Dīn. *Majmu'at al-Rasā'il*, Cairo, 1905

—— *Al-Radd 'ala'l-Manṭiqiyīn*, Bombay, 1949
Ibn Ṭufayl, Abū Bakr. *Ḥayy Ibn Yaqẓān*, Damascus, 1962
Ikhwān al-Ṣafā. *Rasā'il*, 4 vols, Beirut, 1957
al-Jurjāni, 'Abd al-Qādir. *Kitāb al-Ta'rifāt*, Leipzig, 1845
al-Juwayni, Abū'l-Ma'āli. *Kitāb al-Irshād*, Paris, 1938
al-Khayyāt, Abū'l-Ḥusayn. *Kitāb al-Intiṣār*, Beirut, 1957
al-Kindi, Abū Yūsuf. *Rasā'il al-Kindi al-Falsafiyah*, 2 vols, Cairo 1950–3
Kraus, Paul. *Jabīr Ibn Ḥayyān*, Cairo, 1942–3
Miskawayh, Abū 'Ali Aḥmad. *Al-Fawz al-Asghar*, Beirut, 1901
—— *Jawidān Khirad*, or *al-Ḥikmah al-Khālidah*, Cairo, 1952
—— *Tahdhīb al-Akhlāq*, Beirut, 1966
Najib Maḥmud, Zaki. *Tajdīd al-Fikr al-'Arabi*, Beirut, 1971
al-Qifṭi, 'Ali. *Tārikh al-Ḥukamā'*, Leipzig, 1903
al-Qushayri, 'Abd al-Karīm. *Al-Risālah al-Qushayriyah*, Cairo, 1912
—— *Rasā'il Ikhwān al-Ṣafa*, 4 vols, Beirut, 1957
Qutb, Sayyid. *Al-Islām wa Mushkilāt al-Ḥaḍārah*, Cairo, 1963
—— *Ma'ālim fi'l-Ṭarīq*, Cairo, 1962
al-Rāzi, Abū Bakr. *Rasā'il al-Rāzi al-Falsafiyah*, ed. P. Kraus, Cairo, 1939
al-Rāzi, Fakhr al-Dīn. *Al-Mabāḥith al-Mashriqiyah*, Hyderabad, 1924
—— *Al-Muḥaṣṣal*, Cairo, 1905
al-Sahlaji, Abū 'Ali. *Manāqib al-Bistāmi*, in Badawi, *Shaṭaḥāt al-Sūfiyah*
al-Shahrastāni, Abd al-Karīm. *Al-Milal wa'l-Niḥal*, Cairo, 1968
—— *Nihāyat al-Iqdam*, London, 1934
al-Shirāzi, Ṣadr al-Dīn. *Al-Asfār al-Arba'ah*, Tehran, 1865
—— *Kitāb al-Mashā'ir (Livre de penetrations)*, Paris, 1964
—— *Al-Ḥashr wa'l Nushūr*, Cairo, 1984
—— *Rasā'il Akhund Mulla Ṣadra*, Tehran, 1884
al-Sijistāni, Abū Sulayman. *Suwān al-Ḥikmah*, Tehran, 1974
al-Suhrawardi, Shihāb al-Dīn. *Ḥikmat al-Ishrāq*, in *Oeuvres philosophiques et mystiques*, ed. H. Corbin, Tehran and Paris, 1952
—— Talwiḥāt, in *Opera metaphysica et mystica*, ed. H. Corbin, Istanbul, 1945
al-Tawḥīdi, Abū Ḥayyān. *Al-Imtā' wa'l-Mu'ānasah*, Cairo, 1939–44

Works in western languages

Abdel-Kader, A. H. *The Life and Personality of al-Junayd*, London, Luzac, 1962

Adams, C. C. *Islam and Modernism in Egypt*, London, Oxford University Press, 1933

Affifi, A. E. *The Mystical Philosophy of Ibnu'l-'Arabi*, Cambridge, Cambridge University Press, 1938

Afnan, S. M. *Avicenna: His Life and Works*, London, George Allen & Unwin, 1958

'Ali, Amīr. *The Spirit of Islam*, London, Christophers, 1935

Anawati, G. C. *Études de philosophie musulmane*, Paris, J. Vrin, 1974

Anawati, G. C. and L. Gardet. *Introduction à la théologie musulmane*, Paris, J. Vrin, 1948

—— *Mystique musulmane*, Paris, J. Vrin, 1961

al-'Aṭṭās, M. N. *Islam, Secularism and the Philosophy of the Future*, London and New York, Mansell Publishing, 1985

'Awa, A. *L'Esprit critique des Frères de la Pureté*, Beirut, n.p., 1948

Browne, E. G. *Literary History of Persia*, Cambridge, Cambridge University Press, 1924

Corbin, H. *Avicenne et le récit visionnaire*, Paris and Tehran, Departement d'iranologie de l'Institut franco-iranien, 1954

—— *Histoire de la philosophie islamique*, Paris, Gallimard, 1964

Cruz Hernandez, M. *Filiosofia hispano-musulmana*, 2 vols, Madrid, Associacon Española para la progresso de las ciencias, 1964

—— *Abu-l-Walid Ibn Rušd (Averroes)*, Cordoba, Publicationes del Monte de Piedad de Cordoba, 1986

Duhem, P. *Le Système du monde*, Paris, A. Hermann, 1935–59

Fakhry, M. *History of Islamic Philosophy*, London and New York, Columbia University Press, 1983

—— *Philosophy, Dogma and the Impact of Greek Thought in Islam*, Aldershot, Variorum, 1994

—— *Ethical Theories in Islam*, Leiden, Brill, 1994

Gauthier, L. *Ibn Rochd (Averroes)*, Paris, Presses universitaires de Francc, 1948

Gibb, H. A. R. *Modern Trends in Islam*, Chicago, University of Chicago Press, 1945

Gohlman, W. E. *The Life of Ibn Sina*, Albany, State University of New York Press, 1974

Goichon, A. *La Philosophie d'Avicenne et son influence en Europe mediévale*, Paris, n.p., 1944

Goldziher, I. *Introduction to Islamic Theology and Law*, Princeton, Princeton University Press, 1981

Guillaume, A. *The Traditions of Islam*, Oxford, Oxford University Press, 1924

Henry, P. and H. R. Schwyser (eds). *Plotini opera*, Paris and Brussels, Desclée de Brower and L'édition universelle, 1959

Hitti, P. *History of the Arabs*, London, Macmillan, 1953

Hourani, G. (trans.). *Averroes on the Harmony of Religion and Philosophy*, London, Luzac, 1961

—— *Islamic Rationalism: The Ethics of 'Abd al-Jabbār*, Oxford, Clarendon Press, 1971

Iqbal, M. *Reconstruction of Religious Thought in Islam*, Lahore, Muhammad Ashraf, 1951

Khalil Samir, S. and J. S. Nielson (eds). *Christian–Arabic Apologetics during the 'Abbasid Period*, Leiden and New York, Brill, 1994

Kraemer, J. L. *Humanism in the Renaissance of Islam*, Leiden, Brill, 1986

Laoust, H. *Essai sur les doctrines sociales et politiques de T. D. Ahmad b. Taimiya*, Cairo, n.p., 1939

Laroui, A. *L'Idéologie arabe contemporaine*, Paris, F. Maspéro, 1967

—— *La Crise des intellectuels arabes*, Paris, F. Maspéro, 1974

Leaman, O. *Averroes and his Philosophy*, Oxford, Clarendon Press, 1988

McCarthy, R. J. *The Theology of al-Ash'ari*, Beirut, Imprimerie Catholique, 1953

Madkour, I. *L'Organon d'Aristote dans le monde arabe*, Paris, J. Vrin, 1934

Mahdi, M. (trans.). *Al-Farabi's Philosophy of Plato and Aristotle*, Glencoe, Macmillan, 1962

—— *Ibn Khaldūn's Philosophy of History*, London, George Allen & Unwin, 1957

Maimonides, M. *Guide of the Perplexed*, trans. S. Pines, Chicago, University of Chicago Press, 1963

Massignon, L. *Essai sur les origines du lexique technique de la mystique musulmane*, Paris, Paul Geuthner, 1922

—— *La Passion d'al-Hallāj*, Paris, Paul Geuthner, 1922

Mawdūdi, A.-A. *The Moral Foundations of the Islamic Movement*, Lahore, Muhammad Ashraf, 1976

—— *The Islamic Way of Life*, Leicester, The Islamic Foundation, 1986

Mehren, A. F. (ed. and trans.). *Traités mystiques d'Avicenne*, Leiden, Brill, 1889–91

Migne, J.-P. *Patrologia Graeca*, Paris, n.p., 1857–94

Nasr, S. H. *Three Muslim Sages*, Cambridge, Mass., Harvard University Press, 1964

Nasr, S. H. and O. Leaman. *History of Islamic Philosophy*, 2 vols, London and New York, Routledge, 1996

Netton, I. R. *Al-Farābi and his School*, London and New York, Routledge, 1992

Nicholson, R. *Mystics of Islam*, London, Routledge & Kegan Paul, 1914

—— *Studies in Islamic Mysticism*, Cambridge, Cambridge University Press, 1921

Patton, W. M. *Ahmad b. Ḥanbal and the Miḥna*, Leiden, Brill, 1897

Peters, F. E. *Aristotle and the Arabs*, New York, New York University Press, 1968

Pines, S. *Beiträge zur Islamischen Atomenlehre*, Berlin, Greafenhainichen, 1936

Rahman, F. *Avicenna's Psychology*, London, Oxford University Press, 1952

Rénan, E. *Averroes et l'averroïsme*, Paris, Calman Lévy, 1882

Rosenthal, F. (trans.) *Aḥmad b. at-Ṭayyib al-Sarakhsi*, New Haven, American Oriental Society, 1943

—— *The Muqaddimah of Ibn Khaldūn*, New York, The Bolingden Foundation, 1958

Ross, W. D. *Aristotle*, London, Methuen, 1956

Sarton, G., *History of Science*, Cambridge, Mass., Harvard University Press, 1959

Smith, M. *Rābi'a the Mystic*, Cambridge, Cambridge University Press, 1928

—— *Studies in Early Mysticism in the Near and Middle East*, London, Sheldon Press, 1931

Smith, W. C. *Modern Islam in India*, London, Victor Gollancz, 1946

Walzer, R. *Greek into Arabic*, Cambridge, Mass., Harvard University Press, 1962

Walzer, R. and P. Kraus, *Galeni compendium Timaei Platonis*, London, The Warburg Institute, 1951

Walzer, R. and F. Rosenthal. *Alfarabius de Platonis philosophia*, London, The Warburg Institute, 1951

Watt, W. M. *Islamic Philosophy and Theology*, Edinburgh, Edinburgh University Press, 1985

—— *The Formative Period of Islamic Thought*, Edinburgh, Edinburgh University Press, 1973

Wensinck, A. J. *The Muslim Creed*, Cambridge, Cambridge University Press, 1932

—— *La Pensée de Ghazzali*, Paris, Adrien-Maisonneuve, 1940

Wolfson, H. A., *The Philosophy of the Kalam*, Cambridge, Mass., Harvard University Press, 1976

Zaehner, R. C. *Hindu and Muslim Mysticism*, New York, Schocken Books, 1960

Index

A Beginner's Guide to the Baha'i Faith

978-1-85168-563-9
£9.99/ $14.95

This comprehensive study gives anyone interested in the contemporary religious landscape an authoritative insight into this 150-year old tradition, whose spiritual and social teachings are so much in tune with the concerns of today.

Who founded the Baha'i Faith?

What do the Baha'i teachings say will bring us happiness and contentment?

What is the Baha'i view on the purpose of life?

How do Baha'i teachings relate to twenty-first century living?

DR MOOJAN MOMEN has lectured at many universities on topics in Middle Eastern studies and religious studies. He is a Fellow of the Royal Asiatic Society and the author of many books on world religions including *Baha'u'llah: A Short Biography*, also published by Oneworld.

Browse further titles at
www.oneworld-publications.com

Beginners GUIDES

A Beginner's Guide to Christianity

Renowned theologian and bestselling author Keith Ward provides an original and authoritative introduction for those seeking a deeper understanding of this complex faith.

978-1-85168-539-4
£9.99/14.95

"Well ordered and clearly written. Will quickly become a standard textbook." ***Theology***

"An articulate presentation of diverse approaches to Christianity's central concerns … highly recommended." ***Library Journal***

KEITH WARD is Professor of Divinity at Gresham College, London and Regius Professor of Divinity Emeritus, at the University of Oxford. A Fellow of the British Academy and an ordained priest in the Church of England, he has authored many books on the topics of Christianity, faith, and science including the best-selling *God: A Guide for the Perplexed* and *The Case for Religion*, both published by Oneworld.

Browse further titles at
www.oneworld-publications.com

Beginners GUIDES

A Beginner's Guide to Daoism

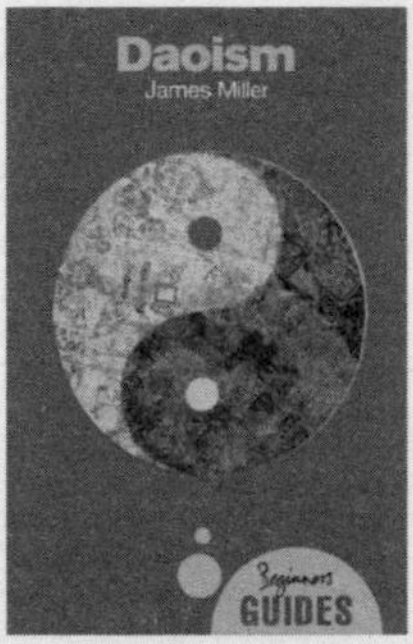

978-1-85168-566-0
£9.99/ $14.95

This informative book will prove invaluable not only to students, but also to general readers who wish to learn more about the origins and nature of a profound tradition, and about its role and relevance in our fast-moving, twenty-first-century existence.

"In this short volume, the author gives his readers not the last word on Daoism but invaluable handles 'to develop your own understanding' of this rich and complex tradition." ***China Review International***

"Just the introductory text we have been waiting for – thoroughly up-to-date, admirably well written, and with an intelligent, and freshly different, thematic organization." **N.J. Girardo** – University Distinguished Professor, Lehigh University

JAMES MILLER is Associate Professor of Chinese Religions at Queen's University, Canada. He is the editor of *Chinese Religions in Contemporary Societies,* and has studied and worked extensively in the Far East.

Browse further titles at
www.oneworld-publications.com

Beginners GUIDES

A Beginner's Guide to Medieval Philosophy

978-1-85168-578-3
£9.99/ $14.95

In this fast-paced, enlightening guide, Sharon M. Kaye takes us on a whistle-stop tour of medieval philosophy, revealing the debt it owes to Aristotle and Plato, and showing how medieval thought is still inspiring philosophers and thinkers today.

"Beautifully written and wonderfully accessible. Discussing all the major thinkers and topics of the period, Kaye's volume does exactly what it should." **William Irwin** – Professor of Philosophy, King's College Pennsylvania and Editor of *The Blackwell Philosophy and Pop Culture Series*

"Simultaneously entices students into and prepares them for the riches of the abundant literature that lies ready for their exploration." **Martin Tweedale** – Professor Emeritus of Medieval Philosophy, University of Alberta

SHARON M. KAYE is Associate Professor of Philosophy at John Carroll University. She is the author of *On Ockham* and *On Augustine.*

Browse further titles at
www.oneworld-publications.com

Beginners GUIDES

A Beginner's Guide to The Qur'an

978-1-85168-624-7
£9.99/ $14.95

Drawing on both contemporary and ancient sources, Esack outlines the key themes and explains the historical and cultural context of this unique work whilst examining its content, language, and style, and the variety of approaches used to interpret it.

"Extremely learned yet accessible, with fascinating insights on virtually every page. Especially useful for those new to the study of Islam, or newly interested in their inherited Islam. Its clarity makes it suitable for undergraduates but its sophistication makes it of interest to graduates as well." **Tamara Sonn** – College of William and Mary, Virginia

"No one has placed the Noble Qur'an more fully in its historical and contemporary context. Esack's is a user's guide for all users, and it should enjoy a long shelf life as the most accessible, and informative, introduction to God's Word in Arabic." **Bruce Lawrence** – Nancy and Jeffrey Marcus Professor of Religion, Duke University

FARID ESACK has an international reputation as a Muslim scholar, speaker, and human rights activist. He has lectured widely on religion and Islamic Studies and also served as a Com missioner for Gender Equality in Nelson Mandela's government.

Browse further titles at
www.oneworld-publications.com

Beginners GUIDES

A Beginner's Guide to Sufism

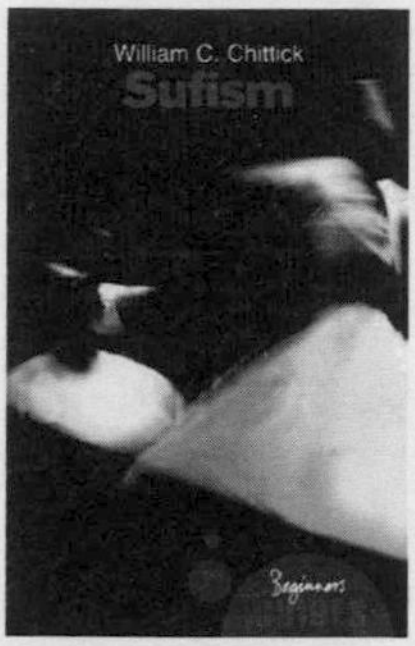

978-1-85168-547-9
£9.99/ $14.95

A compelling insight into the origins, context, and key themes of this fascinating movement.

Fresh and authoritative, this sympathetic book will be appreciated by anyone interested in Sufism, from complete beginners to students, scholars, and experts alike.

"This short book stands out as one of the best books on the subject. A welcome contribution to the study and understanding of Sufism." ***Muslim World Book Review***

"William Chittick is the most exciting writer on Sufism today, combining as he does a genuine passion for the subject with a scholarly objectivity that is truly impressive."
Oliver Leaman – Professor of Philosophy and Zantker Professor of Judaic Studies, University of Kentucky

WILLIAM C. CHITTICK is Professor of Religious Studies at Stony Brook University, New York. He spent over twelve years in Iran before the revolution, and is one of the foremost scholars of Sufism alive today. He is the author and translator of twenty-five books and over one hundred articles on Islamic thought, Sufism, Shi'ism, and Persian Literature.

Browse further titles at
www.oneworld-publications.com

Beginners GUIDES